THE EAST POMERANIAN OFFENSIVE, 1945

CASEMATE | ILLUSTRATED

CASEMATE | ILLUSTRATED

THE EAST POMERANIAN OFFENSIVE, 1945

DESTRUCTION OF GERMAN FORCES IN POMERANIA AND WEST PRUSSIA

IAN BAXTER

CASEMATE | ILLUSTRATED

CIS0043

Published in 2025 by
CASEMATE PUBLISHERS
1950 Lawrence Road, Havertown, PA 19083, USA
and
47 Church Street, Barnsley, S70 2AS, UK

Print Edition: ISBN 978-1-63624-388-7
Digital Edition: ISBN 978-1-63624-389-4

Design by Battlefield Design
Printed and bound in the Czech Republic by FINIDR s.r.o.

CASEMATE PUBLISHERS (US)
Telephone (610) 853-9131
Fax (610) 853-9146
Email: casemate@casematepublishers.com
www.casematepublishers.com

CASEMATE PUBLISHERS (UK)
Telephone (0)1226 734350
Email: casemate@casemateuk.com
www.casemateuk.com

All photos contained in this book are derived from archival sources, including the US National Archives and Records Administration, Library of Congress, Bundesarchiv, and the US Military History Institute, unless otherwise noted.

Author's note: Geographic names are given as they were during World War II and do not reflect current usage.

Acknowledgements: I wish to thank my artist Oliver Missing for his time and expertise in producing some fine and well-detailed German and Russian tanks, including producing the maps. Please find Oliver's vast selection of illustrations at his "Engines of WW2" site: www.o5m6.de (founded in 2003). I also wish to thank my Brazilian soldier artist, Renato Dalmaso, who is an illustrator and comic book artist. He works mainly with watercolor and gouache on paper and illustrates the war comic projects *The Elísio: A Journey to Hell* and *Jambocks*, as well as four comic book albums telling the stories of the Flamengo and São Paulo football clubs. He also works as an illustrator and cover artist for several publications in Europe and Brazil. His email is renatodalmaso@gmail.com.

Title page image: A T-34-85 tank with infantry riders advances along an East Pomeranian road bound for the front.
Contents page map: Soviet spearheads of the 2nd Belorussian Front advance into Pomerania from East Prussia to the Baltic coast.
Contents page image: An SU-76 travels along a cobbled road.
Maps on pages 8, 99 and 114 adapted from the Soviet General Staff's *Prelude to Berlin: The Red Army's Offensive Operations in Poland and Eastern Germany, 1945*. Edited and translated by Richard W. Harrison. Solihull: Helion.

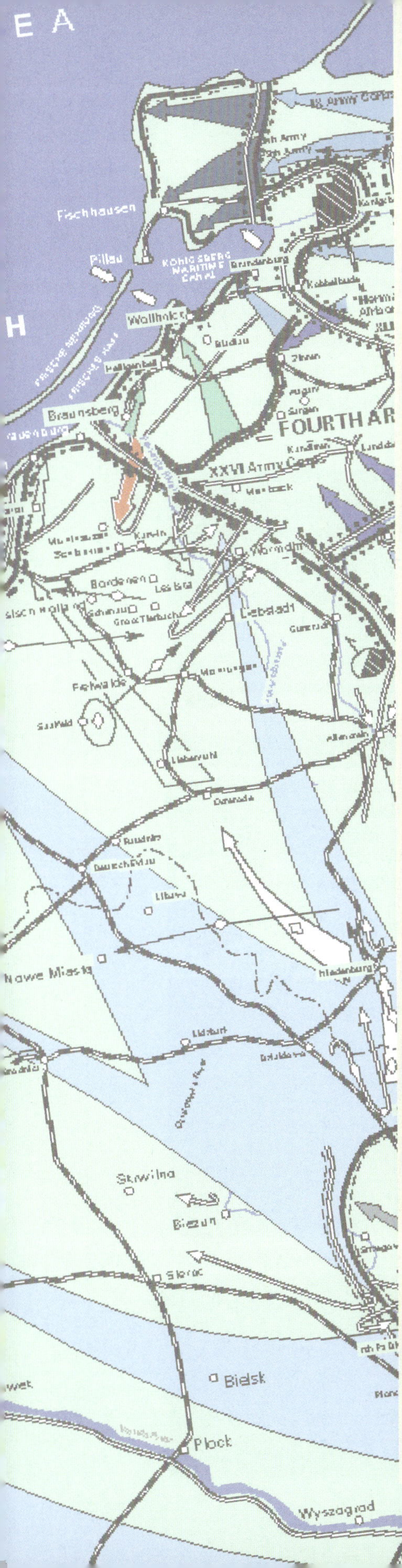
Fischhausen
Pillau
Braunsberg
FOURTH AR
XXVI Army Corps
Nowe Miasto
Skrwilno
Bielsk
Plock
Wyszogrod
Polish 1st Army

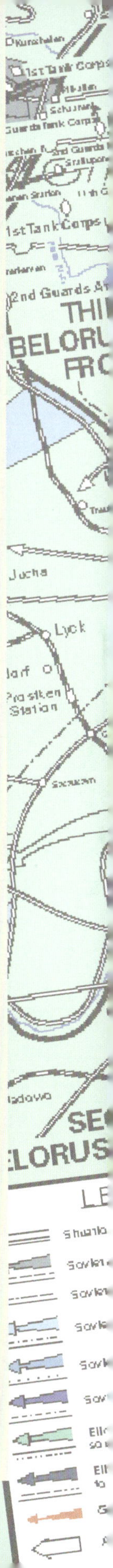
1st Tank Corps
2nd Guards A
THI
BELORU
FRO
Jucha
Lyck
SE
ELORUS

Contents

Timeline of Events

The East Pomeranian offensive was the Soviet precursor to the battle for Berlin that saw the Red Army drive west and north toward the Baltic Sea, crushing enemy resistance and capturing key *Festungen*, or fortresses, such as Kolberg and Danzig. The capture of East Pomerania and the arrival of Soviet formations along the Baltic, securing territory from the Bay of Danzig to the Bay of Stettin, ensured that the northern flank of the Red Army on its drive to Berlin was covered.

January 15, 1945: Soviet winter offensive is launched. Army Group North is attacked by three powerful Soviet fronts: Leningrad, Volkhov, and 2nd Baltic. The German Eighteenth Army bears the brunt of the attack.

January 15, 1945: Soviet offensive begins simultaneously along the Warsaw and Berlin axes in East Prussia, conducted by the 2nd and 3rd Belorussian Fronts.

January 18, 1845: The 2nd and 3rd Belorussian Fronts break through the German defenses in the north, committing their mobile formations and advancing quickly west and north toward the Baltic coast.

January 24, 1945: Following the arrival of the 2nd Belorussian Front at the Baltic and the encirclement of the enemy's East Prussian forces, the Red Army forces the Vistula River and immediately begins an offensive toward East Pomerania. The German 2nd Army is encircled in a massive pincer movement.

January 26, 1945: 2nd Belorussian Front reaches the coast at the Vistula Lagoon, severing land communications with the entire German Fourth Army and several divisions of the Second Army now encircled in the Heiligenbeil Pocket/Cauldron/*Kessel*.

February 1–10, 1945: Stavka, the Soviet Supreme High Command, plans several fronts to operate simultaneously along several axes. The 2nd Belorussian Front is given the objective of cutting off East Prussia and advancing into East Pomerania.

February 24, 1945: Soviet offensive opens against East Pomerania, with the first stage being the Konitz–Koslin offensive operation.

February 27, 1945: Elements of the 2nd Belorussian Front enter East Pomerania and advance toward the Baltic coastal town of Koslin. For two days Soviet troops attack toward Koslin and Konitz, but German resistance is stubborn.

March 1, 1945: 2nd Belorussian Front launches the Arnswalde–Kolberg offensive to run simultaneously with the Danzig offensive. The main objective is Kolberg, a key German position in the "Pomeranian Wall" and a vital link between Pomerania and Prussia.

March 4, 1945: Kolberg is attacked. The garrison is well defended by the Third Panzer Army, 33rd SS Grenadier Division Charlemagne (1st French) and the 15th SS Grenadier Division (1st Latvian), supported by ten thousand *Volkssturm* and Hitlerjugend conscripts and militia volunteers.

March 4, 1945: Koslin falls to the Red Army; the German Second Army is now completely cut off from its army group.

March 6, 1945: 2nd Belorussian Front opens the Danzig offensive, to capture Danzig and Gdingen (Gotenhafen).

March 14, 1945: The Red Army reaches the outskirts of Danzig and advances to the Vistula. 2nd Belorussian Front pounds German Second Army at the Pultusk garrison.

March 18, 1945: Kolberg finally falls and the German defense of East Pomerania begins to disintegrate. When the Poles march into the razed city, they find it almost unrecognizable.

March 18, 1945: 2nd Belorussian Front and Zhukov's 1st Belorussian Front establish the strategic "Kolberg line," from the Oder River estuary to the Schwedt sector. So begins the Altdamm offensive operation.

March 20, 1945: Altdamm falls after tank clashes in the town.

March 25, 1945: 2nd Shock, 65th, 49th, and 19th Armies launch the Danzig offensive. German strength of twenty-four thousand five hundred troops, two hundred AFVs, and five hundred guns face ninety-five thousand five hundred Soviet troops, seven hundred and fifty AFVs, and two thousand five hundred guns.

March 26, 1945: The Germans begin withdrawing armor and artillery from Danzig, pursued by the Soviet 49th Army. German resistance is fanatical as bitter street fighting develops in the suburbs.

March 27, 1945: Soviet troops take Emaus, Danzig's western suburb.

March 31, 1945: German resistance in Danzig collapses as the Red Army assumes total control of the city. Soviet losses are ten thousand men to the Germans' twenty-two thousand, including three thousand captured.

April 4, 1945: The German Second Army is routed.

April 7, 1945: Remnants of the German Second Army and the Fourth Army create the Army East Prussia. Following the fall of Danzig and Gotenhafen, it fights for its very existence in the Bay of Danzig.

A German soldier sits on the edge of his trench armed with a *StG 44*, the German assault rifle. (NARA)

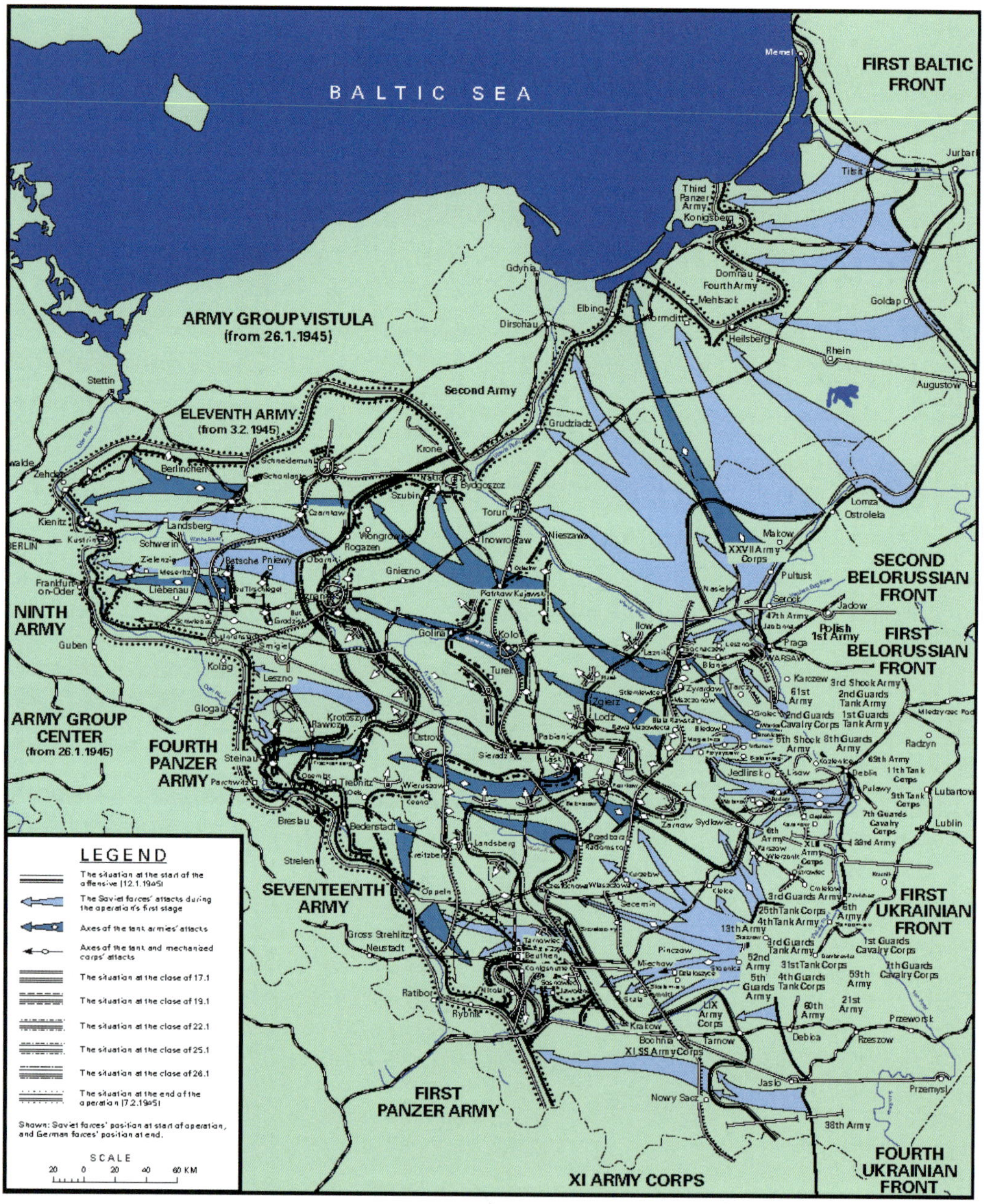

The course of operations (January 12–February 7, 1945).

Introduction: Collapse of Army Group North

By the end of 1943 the strength of the German war machine on the Eastern Front had severely deteriorated. Being outnumbered, continuously short of fuel and ammunition, and having to constantly exert themselves and their machinery to the very limits of endurance was taking its toll. To make matters worse, German units were no longer being refitted with adequate replacements to compensate for their large losses.

Supplies of equipment and ammunition along some sectors of the front were so insufficient that commanders were compelled to ration their men. As a consequence, many soldiers had become increasingly aware that they were in the final stages of fighting the war on Russian soil. Even the battle-hardened Waffen-SS were often starved of important weaponry and machinery. The effect on the experienced and elite formations like the Waffen-SS was a constant concern for the tacticians. These elite units were being used increasingly to help prop up the Eastern Front, and the lack of tanks, artillery and assault guns being

A concerned MG-42 crew wearing the winter white reversible, gray-side-out, take cover in a trench, looking anxiously skyward for enemy aircraft.

A German 8cm Granatwerfer 34 (8cm GrW 34) mortar crew during a fire mission in the snow. This weapon was the standard German infantry mortar throughout the war. It was noted for its accuracy and rapid rate of fire.

rushed to their aid was causing huge problems. This was in stark contrast to the enormous volume of armaments being produced for the Red Army. The Soviets constantly outgunned the Germans; Luftwaffe air support was almost non-existent. Even before the Red Army launched its winter offensive in early 1944 against Army Group North, the front-line German soldier was already continuously under fire from Soviet artillery and aircraft. Ultimately, the German soldier at the end of 1943 was ill prepared to come up against any type of large-scale enemy offensive. As a consequence, both the Waffen-SS and their Wehrmacht counterparts, together with the newly formed Luftwaffe field divisions, were thus faced with the dangerous and worsening prospect of being driven out of Russia and into the Baltic states, where they would have to fight to the death to prevent the Red Army from reaching East Prussia and East Pomerania.

On January 15, 1944, German Army Group North was attacked by three powerful Soviet fronts, the Leningrad, Volkhov, and 2nd Baltic. The German Eighteenth Army,

Grenadiers inside the cab of an Sd.Kfz. 251 halftrack personnel carrier using an 8cm GrW 34 against an enemy target.

which bore the brunt of the attacks, was outnumbered by at least 3:1 in divisions. For days Soviet ground bombardments pounded the Germans, reducing German defenses to small, isolated pockets of resistance. These heavy attacks were supported by repeated Soviet aerial bombardments which allowed Soviet infantry to break through enemy lines and capture large swaths of enemy territory. As usual German troops were expected to hold the front, but overwhelming enemy firepower proved too much for Küchler's Army Group North and it was compelled to fall back under a hurricane of enemy fire.

On January 26 the city of Leningrad was liberated after 900 days of siege. The German Eighteenth Army was now split into three and struggled to maintain any type of front forward of the Luga River. Over the coming weeks the Soviets began exerting more pressure, especially against the Sixteenth Army defending positions along the Baltic. But the spring thaw arrived early and melting snow turned the roads on which the Soviets were traveling into a quagmire, slowing their advance.

Although the Germans had been given some reprieve from the Soviet onslaught, the Baltic states were now threatened, despite German units being ordered to fanatically hold their positions. This threat became reality when the Red Army launched their long-awaited Operation *Bagration* against Army Group Center on June 22, 1944, which destroyed 17 German divisions in a matter of weeks. Along the Narva Front, German infantry divisions bitterly contested large areas of countryside. Fighting was often savage, resulting in terrible casualties on both sides.

However, despite dogged resistance and determination to hold the German lines to the grim death, the annihilation of Army Group Center meant that much of the pressure now fell on Army Group North. By mid-July the Red Army had already taken full advantage of the situation and was slowly grinding down the German forces in Estonia and Lithuania. On July 13 the Lithuanian capital of Vilnius fell, and a few weeks later Narva was captured, which allowed Soviet spearheads to advance northwest and capture the Estonian capital, Tallinn.

A column of Sturmgeschütz roll through a town, destined for the front. The town appears unscathed.

A 15cm howitzer in action. Throughout the war this weapon was extensively used by the Wehrmacht.

By the end of September 1944, Army Group North was strategically in a critically dangerous position. The front was badly scarred and depleted, and the bulk of its forces had withdrawn from Estonia; it was already being threatened in Latvia and Lithuania. As the threat of Soviet attacks into the Baltic states increased, the Pomeranian Wall/Line, known as the *Die Pommernstellung*, was renovated and strengthened by the Germans. This line of old concrete fortifications had been built in the early 1930s in the Pomeranian Lakeland as a light defensive position in case of an attack by the Second Polish Republic against the German republic. It stretched from Landsberg an der Warthe to Baldenburg. Although it was believed that this defensive line would not prevent a heavy Soviet attack, it was hoped that it would slow the Red Army advance and cause massive casualties.

As the Pomeranian Wall was being renovated with underground tunnels and heavy antitank, artillery, and machine-gun positions, the Red Army continued its remorseless advance. On October 9, 1944, Soviet spearheads reached the Baltic Sea near Memel after overrunning the headquarters of the German Third Panzer Army. As a result, Army Group

Wehrmacht soldiers in their familiar splinter army smocks sit around a campfire during a lull in the fighting.

North was cut off from East Prussia, which angered Hitler bitterly. He was urged to evacuate the troops from the area to stabilize the front and prop up defenses in East Prussia. The Führer refused and ordered some thirty-three divisions to deploy to the Kurland area where they were ordered to dig in and fight to the death to defend what remained of the Latvian territory still in German hands. Hitler's refusal to evacuate Army Group North resulted in the entrenchment of more than two hundred thousand German troops, mainly from the 18th and 16th Armies, in what was to become known to the Germans as the Kurland Bridgehead.

Undeterred by massive losses, the Red Army launched the Riga offensive; the Latvian capital fell on October 24. From October 27 to November 25, Soviet units launched an offensive to break through the front toward Skrunda and Saldus. The attack was so powerful that along parts of the front the Red Army employed some fifty-two divisions simultaneously against the Germans.

By the beginning of 1945 the German war machine on the Eastern Front had been significantly weakened, having suffered massive losses. When the Red Army launched its long-awaited winter offensive along a thousand-mile front spanning from the Baltic Sea to the Carpathian Mountains against German Army Groups Center and A, the objective was an all-out assault against the Nazi capital Berlin. Of the 83 German divisions defending the front lines, 12 were panzer and panzergrenadier. Some forty percent of all German forces had been thrown into the Eastern Front to defend East Prussia, Pomerania, Warsaw, Berlin, and the Silesian industrial heartland.

Civilians pressed into service dig miles of antitank ditches to slow the Soviet advance from East Prussia along the Baltic coast and into Pomerania.

Wehrmacht troops, engineers, and Todt construction workers building one of the many defensive positions in the Army Group North zone of operations. One of the largest sets of fortifications was the Pomeranian Wall, a line of defenses to keep open the vital link between Pomerania and Prussia.

The Soviet offensive began simultaneously along the East Prussian, Warsaw, and Berlin axes. Its powerful forces conducted strong offensive operations in close strategic coordination in East Prussia using the 2nd and 3rd Belorussian Fronts. Its objective was to prevent the enemy's defensive plan from unfolding along the main strategic direction, stemming the enemy's maneuver of operational and strategic reserves to reinforce its forces along the Warsaw–Berlin axis. Stavka, the Soviet Supreme High Command, had planned and organized several fronts which were to operate along several directions and achieve simultaneous objectives using several offensive stages to destroy the enemy. The offensives were all about keeping the battlefield moving and subjecting the Germans to massive

A Soviet SU-152 belonging to the 2nd Baltic Front advancing through a forest.

ongoing attacks. The 2nd and 3rd Belorussian Fronts were given the important objective of first cutting off East Prussia and preventing the Germans from reinforcing it. Following successful operations in East Prussia the Soviet fronts would defeat and destroy the entire northern strategic wing of the German front. The 2nd Belorussian Front would then begin large, sweeping attacks aimed at cutting off East Prussia and the German forces there from the rest of Germany by simultaneously launching deep frontal attacks towards the city of Königsberg. The whole plan was to split the East Prussian forces into parts, surround them, and then annihilate them.

The Soviet offensive in the north saw both the 2nd and 3rd Belorussian Fronts break through the German defenses, committing their mobile formations and quickly developing successful, deep penetrations. The 2nd Belorussian Front had committed powerful mobile formations, which saw the rapid destruction of German forces along the Przasnysz–Mlawa line. Further attacks were made toward the Baltic coast where they were able to cut off the Germans' paths of retreat from East Prussia. Massed tanks supported by aerial bombardment meant that the Soviet spearheads were able to quickly advance and destroy all enemy centers of resistance in their path. They also decisively suppressed German efforts to launch counterattacks or properly organize a cohesive defense.

Following the 2nd Belorussian's arrival at the Baltic Sea and the encirclement of the enemy's East Prussian group of forces, the Red Army forced the Vistula River and immediately began an offensive westward in the direction of East Pomerania. Whilst its forces attacked along the Baltic Coast, plans had already been drawn up for an East Pomeranian operation.

Over the days that ensued in February 1945, fighting in the Baltics raged with unabated ferocity as German and Latvian troops waged an unprecedented battle of attrition against an overwhelming enemy strength, attempting to stall the massive Soviet push toward East Pomerania with the remaining weapons and men they had at their disposal. Hitler told his front-line commanders of the significance of losing the Baltics; it would mean that all

Two crewmembers stand next to their stationary Nashorn panzerjäger during a lull in the fighting, January 1945. This tank killer was well suited to the open, flat terrain.

coastal garrisons would be cut off. He made it quite clear that all remaining Wehrmacht and Waffen-SS units were not to evacuate, but to stand and fight to the death. He was determined to prevent the Red Army from spilling out into the Baltic states, capturing East and West Prussia, taking the ancient Teutonic city of Danzig, and driving its mighty forces into the heartland of East Pomerania. What Hitler was trying to avoid was a desperate defense along the frontier of the Reich. Instead, he wanted to draw as much of the main Soviet force away from its concerted effort toward Berlin. It was for this reason that the Führer made it known to his commanders in the field that their troops would have to defend their fortified positions with every drop of their blood if they were to avert a complete disaster on the Eastern Front.

Very young Hitlerjugend troops in Lauban, Poland, 1945.

German troops relax in a defensive position east of Danzig, mid-February 1945.

This was to be Hitler's last defensive measure in the north and northwest, and it would be in East and West Prussia, Danzig, and East Pomerania, where his troops would have to fight to save their homeland from a Soviet invasion.

The strategic results of the Red Army's winter offensive in early 1945 were truly enormous. The Germans suffered a heavy blow and were soon defeated along a broad front stretching from the Baltic Sea to the Carpathians. Soviet spearheads had managed to advance some three hundred and fifty miles in 17 days in January, and they'd reached the Oder River to prepare its forces for an advance on Berlin. The German East Prussian forces had been cut off and were subsequently all but destroyed. Stalin's strategy was a masterstroke. The planning was brilliant, and involved the operational coordination of neighboring fronts, especially between the 2nd and 3rd Belorussian Fronts.

With Soviet success against German forces in the north, the overall Soviet military-political situation now dictated the necessity for the preparation of a final attack in the direction of Berlin. It was for this reason, and to securely guard the right wing of the Red Army advancing on Berlin, that Stalin needed the German defensive positions to be eliminated first in East Pomerania.

Well-clad German artillerymen prepare their 15cm gun, 1945.

| German Forces

Even at the start of the German invasion of the Soviet Union in June 1941, German front-line commanders were amazed at the strategic situation on the ground. By the end of the summer of that year, German armies were already beginning to stall along certain parts of the front and were overextending their lines due to the vastness of the Russian steppes. Soldiers had found the land so immense and ever widening that some operations could only be conducted successfully in certain areas.

As a result, as the war progressed, it was realized that the German front could not be maintained. Instead, sizable gaps had to be regularly filled in major German units. The mobility differences between motorized and non-motorized elements of the Wehrmacht caused the Germans to advance in very different ways and at different speeds. The extended distances over which the Germans were operating continuously caused growing problems, which meant that often tanks outstripped the following infantry. This consequently caused spaces to open up between German units, and Soviet forces were able to exploit these gaps by successfully counterattacking. However, the German leadership continued by arguing that strategy would prevail on the Eastern Front, whilst the Soviets demonstrated that they could, in fact, exploit the German front by attacking the large gaps that had developed between subunits and even the divisions. By 1944, the problem had escalated further for the Germans as the gaps along the front continued to widen. As a result, German formations found themselves locked in desperate defensive combat, with many of the infantry and panzer divisions unable to establish an elastic defense in depth due to extended frontages and a severe shortage of reserves. Agitated and angered by the growing problems along the front, Hitler frantically began ordering mobile units stripped from other sectors to deal with this new emergency. However, it was too late. The Germans were constantly outmaneuvered and their reserves stretched to the limit. Coupled with huge logistical problems, including dire shortages of fuel, ammunition, and food, many units could not sustain themselves adequately, and as a result the front cracked and receded. The road system also posed a major problem for armored vehicles, and the lack of field maintenance crews meant that tank crews often had to abandon their machines.

As operations further progressed in Army Group North in 1944, it was clear that the present disposition and line of the German front was in no way suited for sustained defense. With the front already overstretched and fighting overwhelming numbers of enemy troops, there were insufficient forces available to create defensive depth, with no reserves ready for any type of successful counterattack. Hitler had already stripped Army Group North of most of its mobile divisions to support Army Group Center's counterattacks during the Soviet *Bagration* summer offensive: Hitler had fallen for an outrageous Stavka ploy, unaware that Army Group North was the next principal target. As a result, the German divisions that were slowly withdrawing into the Baltic states had become overextended and were lacking

In Profile:
Heer Sentry and MG-42 Machine Gunner, January/February 1945

This sentry has not been fortunate enough to receive his winter uniform due to severe shortages. His M35 steel helmet has a white cloth covering and is held in place by a leather strap. He wears the standard German infantryman's greatcoat, standard wool gloves, and the woolen toque around his neck to keep him warm. He is armed with the standard Karbiner 98k bolt-action rifle and wears an infantryman's black leather belt with carbine pouches attached. (Renato Dalmaso)

An MG-42 machine gunner in early February 1945. He wears the Heer parka white-side-out. His standard infantryman's black leather belt carries a late war issued MG-34/42 tool pouch or *MG Werkzeugtasche* and black P38 hardshell holster for his Walther P38 pistol. His field-gray trousers are tucked into his black leather boots protected by puttees. By 1944 chronic leather shortages caused the German army to adopt puttees in place of the knee-high leather boots initially worn. (Renato Dalmaso)

In Profile: Mittlerer Schützenpanzerwagen (7.5cm) (Sd.Kfz. 251/9) and Volkswagen Type 82 Kübelwagen, Second Army, February 1945

This XXXXVI Panzer Corps Sd.Kfz. 251/9 halftrack armed with the powerful 7.5cm gun was initially developed as a support vehicle for motorized infantry. For local defense the vehicle mounts the MG-42 machine gun. Due to lack of paint, it has been given a sparse coating of whitewash over its summer camouflage scheme. (Oliver Missing)

This XXIII Corps light utility vehicle was found in all panzer and infantry divisions during the war. It was designed to be to be driven at low speed to keep pace with marching infantry. The vehicle has received a full coating of winter whitewash. (Oliver Missing)

any kind of depth. German front lines were more often a hodge-podge of strongpoints than a continuous line of defense. Along many parts of the German front, the lines were so fluid because of the Soviet speed of advance that the German front consisted mostly of a thin line of disconnected rifle pits. Consequently, there were no proper defenses, and those that were erected were often built hastily and were unable to sustain prolonged enemy attack. Soviet firepower was overwhelming and often German troops were stuck in their foxholes or trenches, unable to move until nightfall. As a result of these conditions, Army Group North paid an extremely high price in blood. With many of these losses irreplaceable, the German ability to seize and hold terrain collapsed. Furthermore, by early 1945, there were huge shortages of front-line officers, who were often too overstretched to implement orders or plan tactically.

Yet, Hitler still did not regard the strategic problems in a traditional manner, despite the impending doom of his army. In the German dictator's mind, the prestige value of holding key areas and cities often outweighed any risk that German forces might have to endure to hold it. Instead, Hitler had to watch the disintegration of the German front, but convinced himself that he could still enthuse further determination into his troops to defend their positions to the bitter end. In fact, Hitler sent a "Fortified Area" order to his front-line commanders in March 1945 to create *festen plätze*, or fortified places, across the Eastern Front. Individual towns or cities that he declared as fortresses were expected to fight to the death rather than retreat or surrender. The "stronghold" was Hitler's dramatic response to the failed defensive strategy on the Eastern Front which he himself had initially instigated. With no reinforcements or equipment to help his beleaguered soldiers, defensive strategy now relied squarely on where Hitler stabbed his finger on the map. His theory was that, even if the fortified areas were encircled, the stronghold would draw in enough Soviet formations to make the loss of men worthwhile. In the end, the German defensive strategy was about sacrificing hundreds of thousands of soldiers to drain Soviet resources to prevent the Red Army marching into Germany.

German Order of Battle, March 1, 1945

Army Group Vistula

Army	Corps	Division
Reserves: Staff Eleventh Army		Div.-Staff zbV 610, bulk Police Div. Silesia
Ninth Army (Reserves: 10 SS-Pz.Div. Frundsberg)	V SS Mountain	Div.-Staff zbV 391, 32 SS-Panzer-Div. '30. Jan.', Div.-Staff Regemer (433 and 463 Inf.Div.), Fortress Frankfurt
	XI SS	712 Inf.Div., Panzer Group Kurmark, 25 Pz.Gren.Div., Fortress Küstrin

Army	Corps	Division
	CI	Infantry Div. Berlin, Infantry Div. Döberitz, Div.-Staff zbV 606
	Corps Oder (directly subordinated to the Army Group)	1 Navy Rifle Div., Groupe Obern... [*illegible in the original*], Group Klessek
Third Panzer Army (Reserves: bulk 33 SS-Gren.Div. Charlemagne, Pz.Div. Holstein)	Defense Area Oder (deputy II Army Corps)	9 Paratroopers Div., Group Deneke
	III SS Panzer	261 Inf.Div., 11 SS-Volunteers Gren.Div. Nordland, 28. SS Volunteers Gren.Div. Wallonien, Grenadiers Group Voigt, 27 SS-Div. Langemarck, 23 SS-Pz. Gren.Div. Nederland
	X SS	5 Jäger, 163 Inf.Div., Div.Staff zbV 402
	Corps Group Tettau	Operational Division Bärewalde, Operational Division Pommerland, elements 33 SS-Div., Latvian (Nr.1) SS-Gren.Div., remains 15 Inf.Div.
Second Army (with deputy XX Corps staff and fortress Graudenz; Reserves: Replacements Brigade Fallschirm-Pz. Div. Hermann Göring, LV Corps staff, remains of 203 and 549 Inf.Div., bulk 547 Inf.Div.)	VII Panzer	4 SS-Polizei-Pz.Gren.Div., 7 Panzer-Div.
	XVIII Mountain	32, 215 Inf.Div.
	XXXXVI Panzer	227, 389 Inf.Div., 4 Panzer-Div., Blocking Brigade 1
	XXVII	251 Inf.Div., Group 73 Inf.Div., elements 31 Inf.Div.
	XXIII	542 VG, 23, 35, 83, 232, 357 Inf.Div.
	Corps Group von Rappard	7 Inf.Div., Group Gumpel

Army Group North

Army	Corps	Division
Fourth Army	Commander Frische Nehrung	Staff 129 Inf.Div.
	XXVI	14 Inf.Div, 349 (Keets) Inf.Div., 28 Jäger-Div., 24 Panzer-Div., remnants 299 Inf.Div.
	VI	Battle Groups 61, 131, 541 Inf. Div., 18 Pz.Gren.Div., 10 Cyclists Jäger-Brigade

Army	Corps	Division
	XX	Battle Groups 21, 102, 292, 558 Inf.Div., remnants 120 Inf.Div.
	XXXXI Panzer	Battle Group Hauser, Div.-Staff zbV 605, 56 Inf.Div., Battle Group 170 Inf.Div.
	Fallschirm-Panzer (armored paratroopers) Corps Hermann Göring (HG)	2 Fallschirm-Panzer-Div. HG, Pz.Gren.Div. Grossdeutschland, 50 Inf.Div., 562 VG
	Fortress commander Königsberg	367 Inf.Div., 561 VG, Battle Group 69 Inf.Div.
Army Detachment Samland (Reserves: staff XXVIII Corps, 5 Panzer-Div., battle group 1 Inf.Div.)	IX	Fortress commander Pillau (Div.-Staff zbV 607), Div.-Staff 548 VG, 58, 93, 95 Inf.Div., Battle Group 551 VG, remnants 286 Inf.Div.

Army Group Kurland

Army	Corps	Division
Reserves		201 Security Div., Staff Field trainings Div. Kurland
Eighteenth Army with fortress commander Libau (fortress staff 52 Security Div.)	Reserves	12, 14 Panzer-Div., Battle Group 121 Inf. Div.
	X	30, 87 Inf.Div., 12 Luftwaffen Field Div., Battle Group 126 Inf.Div.
	I	132, 218 Inf.Div.
	L	11, 205, 225 Inf.Div.
	II	263 Inf.Div., 563 VG, Battle Group 290 Inf.Div.
Sixteenth Army	XXXVIII Panzer	122, 329 Inf.Div.
	VI SS Volunteers	24 Inf.Div., 19 (Latvian No. 2) SS-Grenadier-Div.
	XVI	81 Inf.Div., Div. zbV 300, Staff 21 Luftwaffen Field (Barth)
	XXXXIII	commander coast (F.K. 186), Group East, Staff Security Div. zbV 207, Group North, Group Northwest, fortress commander Windau, Group Southwest

(Information taken from original order of battle, author's collection)

In Profile:

Marder II Panzerjäger, Panzer Division Holstein and Maultier Sd.Kfz. 3b, 27th SS Volunteer Grenadier Division Langemarck, Altdamm, March 1945

This whitewashed Waffen-SS Marder II Panzerjäger saw defensive action around Kolberg and then in front of Altdamm, with Army Group Vistula. Panzer Division Holstein incurred heavy losses and its remnants were slowly absorbed by the 18th Volksgrenadier Division which was supported by a handful of Panzerjägers. (Oliver Missing)

This 9th Flak Company V3000S/SSM Maultier (Mule) is based on the Ford V3000S with a tracked suspension system based on the British Universal Carrier. The platform was subsequently modified for other uses, including as an antiaircraft halftrack by mounting a 2cm Flak 38 on the flatbed for air defense. The vehicle is lightly painted in winter whitewash; its summer camouflage scheme can clearly still be seen. (Oliver Missing)

General Walter-Otto Weiß, shown second from left in this photo.

German Commanders

Second Army

General Walter-Otto Weiß, second from left in photo (September 5, 1890–December 21, 1967)

Walter Weiß was born into a family of farmers and officers who immigrated to East Prussia at the end of the 18th century. Weiß was a strategist and a confident, able, high-ranking soldier. His confidence and courage were his undoing, as he frequently opposed Hitler and often voiced his objections. In front of his men Weiß was respected, and on the battlefield and during military briefings he was a man who was very familiar with war tactics and defense. From February 4, 1943 to March 9, 1945, he was commander-in-chief of the Second Army. On January 30, 1944, he was promoted to colonel general. That year the Second Army survived the Soviet summer *Bagration* offensive in June 1944 due to Weiß strategically withdrawing his units from being encircled and destroyed. In January 1945 his army was subordinated to the newly formed Army Group Vistula. Fighting was bitter and Weiß once again demonstrated his ability to defend and tactically withdraw to save his forces. His defensive skills led to him being entrusted with building a new front on the lower Vistula to protect the Bay of Danzig, which was being threatened by Soviet spearheads that were preparing their East Pomeranian offensive operation. During the battle of East Pomerania, the Second Army lost considerable ground and their new front buckled under the weight of the Soviet onslaught. Despite frequent requests by the general to withdraw his forces, Hitler was adamant they must stay where they were and fight. What followed were constant calls from Weiß warning Hitler of the serious consequences of the situation. In the Heiligenbeil Pocket, where fighting had been raging since January, Weiß threatened to pull his army out before it was destroyed. As a result, on March 9, he was relieved of his command and replaced by General Dietrich von Saucken. As predicted, the replacement did not prevent the Second Army from withdrawing in panic and confusion to Danzig and Gdingen, where they were besieged by 2nd Belorussian Front.

Second Panzer Army

General Dietrich Friedrich Eduard Kasimir von Saucken (May 16, 1892–September 27, 1980)

Saucken personified the archetypal aristocratic Prussian conservative who was not a Nazi. He was often critical of the Nazi military leadership and was deeply critical of National Socialism and Adolf Hitler's

(BA 101I-088-3724-06A)

ability to lead his forces onto a battlefield. As a military commander, he demonstrated a tendency towards self-promotion coupled with tactical and aggressive brilliance. He was a great panzer commander on the Eastern Front, which earned him respect among his *panzertruppen*. It would not be until March 1945 that he took command of the Second Army in Prussia and provided logistical support for the evacuation of forces from East Prussia. In early April the remnants of his Second Army were absorbed into the newly formed Army East Prussia. With the war lost, Saucken received notice on May 8 that he had been awarded the Knight's Cross with Oak Leaves, Swords and Diamonds, making him the last officer to receive this award. Even with the Red Army approaching, Saucken, like a typical Prussian, would not be evacuated, preferring to stay with his troops until they surrendered the following day, on May 9, 1945.

Third Panzer Army

General Erhard Raus (January 8, 1889–April 3, 1956)

General Raus was an Austrian-born commander who rose steadily through the ranks. On the battlefield he was a well-respected panzer leader. Initially a brigade commander with the 6th Panzer Division, in June 1941 his tactical and strategic brilliance led to a string of successes. He quickly learned tactics under fire and even as the German military situation deteriorated, he performed brilliantly on the strategic defensive. In late December 1943 he was given the command of the Fourth Panzer Army. In 1944 he took command of the First Panzer Army and then the Third Panzer Army, which included the III Panzer Corps, XI SS Corps, and Corps Group Tettau. In February 1945, Hitler ordered Raus to take command of the XI SS Panzer Corps in East Pomerania and use his wealth of experience to hold the line against the Soviet onslaught. However, when Raus began a strategic withdrawal to save his army from destruction, the Führer sacked him, accusing him of being weak, making poor decisions, and allowing the enemy to cross the frontier into Germany.

X SS Corps

General Günther Krappe (April 13, 1893–December 31, 1981)

Delegated with the leadership of the X Waffen-SS Corps between February 10 and March 6, 1945.

III SS Panzer Corps

General Martin Unrein (January 2, 1901–January 22, 1972)

Commanded the III Waffen-SS Panzer Corps between February 11 and March 5, 1945.

III SS Panzer Corps

General Felix Martin Julius Steiner (May 23, 1896–May 12, 1966)

Given command of the III Waffen-SS Corps between March 5 and May 8, 1945.

VII Panzer Corps

General Mortimer von Kessel (May 25, 1893–January 8, 1981)

In December 1944, Kessel was given the leadership of the VII Panzer Corps, which operated in East Prussia and East Pomerania in February and March 1945. He surrendered to the Soviets in May 1945.

XVIII Mountain Corps

General Friedrich Hochbaum (August 7, 1894–January 28, 1955)

On June 24, 1944, Hochbaum was given the leadership of the XVIII Mountain Corps and, with his promotion to general of the infantry, was appointed commanding general on September 1, 1944. He operated in East Pomerania in February and March 1945 and surrendered to the Soviets in May 1945.

XXVII Army Corps

General Maximilian Felzmann (April 22, 1894–June 8, 1962)

In October 1944, Felzmann took command of the XXVII Army Corps. By the time it was used for defensive operations in East Pomerania, it had been rebuilt and transferred to the Second Army. During the offensive, it was encircled on the Baltic coast at Danzig, and again destroyed/disbanded. Felzmann was relieved of his command in April 1945 and what was left of the corps was put under the command of General Walter Hornlein. Hornlein and his staff were evacuated and transferred to the reconstructed Third Panzer Army, and the remnants of the corps eventually surrendered to U.S. Army troops on May 4.

XXXXVI Panzer Corps

General Martin Gareis (October 6, 1891–February 26, 1976)

Gareis was delegated with the leadership of XXXXVI Panzer Corps between January 19 and May 3, 1945. Under his command the corps tactically withdrew through 1945 into Poland and ended the war fighting defensively in East Pomerania. Much of the corps was annihilated; by the end of April 1945, only the 547th Volksgrenadier Division and the 2nd Naval Division were still standing.

XXIII Army Corps

General Walter Melzer (October 7, 1894–June 23, 1961)

Appointed commander of the XXIII Army Corps in October 1944 until he surrendered on May 8, 1945.

Soviet Forces

The Soviets politically and geographically saw the Baltic region as part of their own, just as the Russians did in the time of Peter the Great. When the Soviets were forced out of the Baltics in 1941 during the German invasion of the Soviet Union, Stalin was determined to reoccupy the region one day. Three years later, in 1944, after Soviet forces broke out from the Leningrad pocket, Stalin made it known to his Anglo-American allies that when the Nazis were expelled from the Baltic region, it would fall under Soviet control.

For this reason, all available forces were to be used against German Army Group North to spearhead powerful formations through the Baltics, testing the Germans everywhere for weaknesses. Once the Baltics were under Soviet control, all available resources were to be sent through to East and West Prussia and East Pomerania. The Red Army was now fully on the offensive. To bring about their success in the region they adopted a series of strategies, including the creation of shock troop units to destroy withdrawing enemy forces. Also, special mobile detachments were formed to pursue the retreating Germans when the front buckled and caved in. All this was supported by the powerful Red Army Air Force. It was also paramount for the Red Army to use the terrain, natural obstacles, and weather to their advantage.

The offensive plan would be undertaken in a series of phases but could only be executed and achieved based on the serviceability of the tracked and wheeled vehicles. Armored or motorized divisions were needed to keep the Germans off balance and to seize important towns and cities as the Soviets thrust deep into enemy territory.

One of the most important concepts of the offensive was attacking in-depth to stem enemy concentrations and overwhelm any pockets of resistance. Massing their aircraft, the Soviets would first gain and then maintain air superiority and begin attacking ground targets with waves of aircraft to achieve vital positions and slowly pulverize the enemy into submission. Doctrinally, the Soviets were as ready for war as the Germans, but initially there was a stark difference in their performance on the battlefield. The German war machine was tactically and strategically more advanced in preparation for fighting than their "Red foe." The Soviets, however, had to evolve on the battlefield. Between 1941 and 1942 their army was generally fighting a defensive war of attrition. By late 1943 the Soviets felt confident in their ability to survive, and slowly and inexorably went on the offensive. As a result, the Wehrmacht was ground down and began taking up a defensive strategy of its own as the tables were slowly turned. The Germans not only began fighting to save one position after another, but were further weakened by climatic conditions, and ultimately destroyed by the overpowering might of the Red Army.

In Profile: Soviet Rifleman and Female Sniper

This Soviet rifleman is resting on freshly cut logs and drinking from a cup during a pause in his regiment's advance. His Ssh-40 steel helmet is next to him, along with an accordion. He wears the Soviet *uschanka* winter fur hat and is dressed in the M35 uniform with black leather combat boots and puttees. (Renato Dalmaso)

Over two thousand Soviet women were trained as sharpshooters and deployed to some of the most dangerous battlegrounds, far from their units, where they were required to lie still for hours to avoid detection in order to kill their target. This sniper is armed with the Mosin–Nagant infantry rifle, complete with optical sight. She wears the *pilotka* hat and over her uniform a *plash-palatka* rain/tent coat. (Renato Dalmaso)

In Profile:

PPSh-41 Submachine Gunner and Dyagterev DP-27 M1940 Machine Gunner

A Soviet submachine gunner wearing black woolen gloves reloads his PPSh-41 drum magazine. He wears the standard winter Soviet jacket and pants: *telogreika* (Soviet body warmer) and *fufaika* (winter outwear). Attached to his leather belt is the PPSh-41 magazine pouch. Protecting his head, he wears the SSh-40 steel helmet with woolen toque. (Renato Dalmaso)

The DP-27 machine gunner wears the standard infantryman's greatcoat. Unusually he wears the *pilotka* hat which was worn during the summer season instead of the winter *ushanka*. Attached to his greatcoat belt is his entrenching tool and flask. Not visible are his ammunition pouches. (Renato Dalmaso)

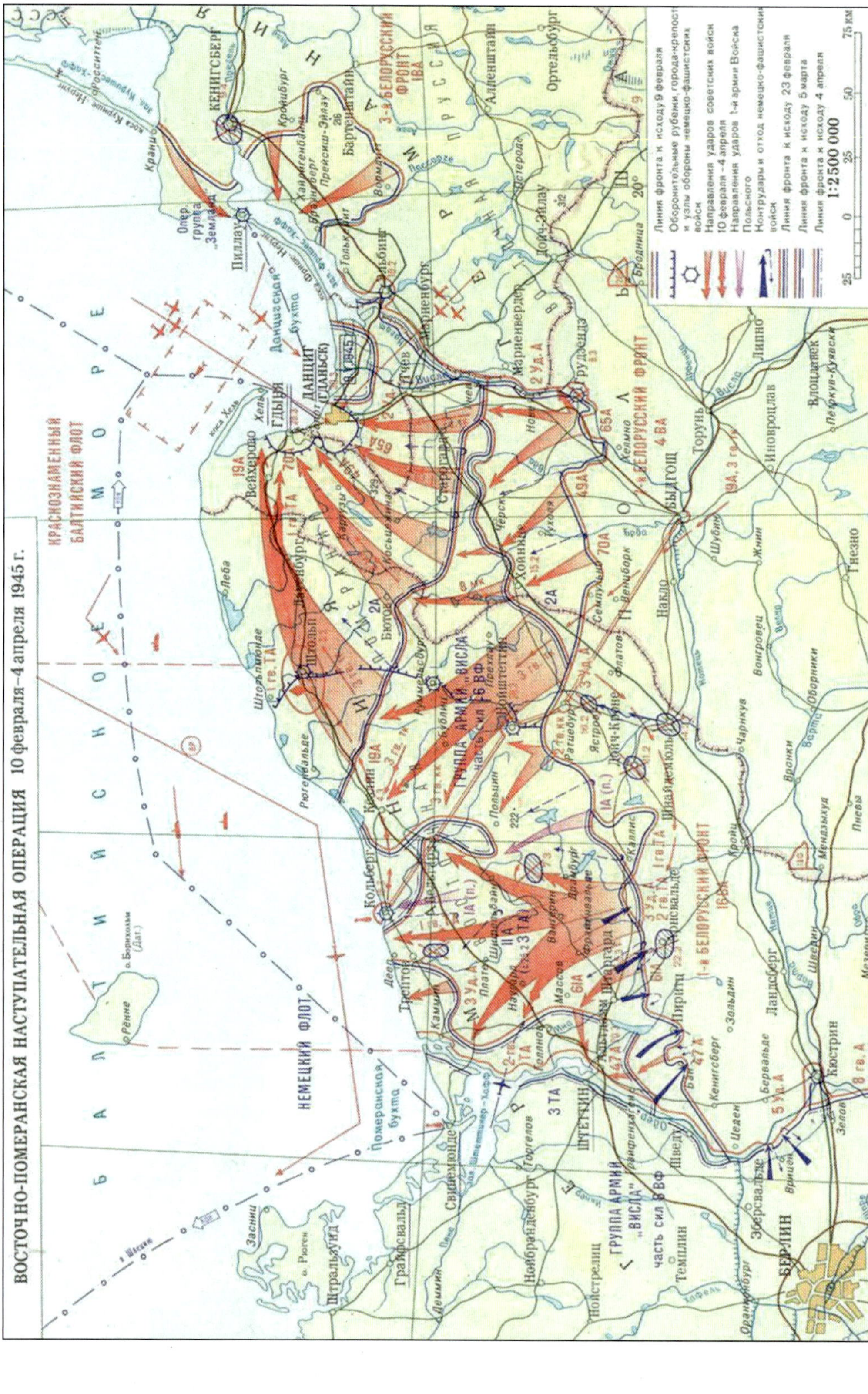

A Soviet map showing the disposition of Red Army forces moving into East Prussia and Pomerania.

The Soviets saw the use of tactical combat power purely as a tool for fragmenting enemy formations. Once German positions were destroyed, the Red Army then had to disrupt the movement of additional German forces, such as by hampering the movement of reserves to the front. Before any attack, massed artillery was launched first in conjunction with limited ground attacks where Soviet formations probed enemy defenses to determine composition, disposition, and strength. Through 1944, German commanders were fully aware of the worsening position on the front. They knew they were not only massively outnumbered in men and equipment, but that they were also overstretched and lacked proper reserves. Communication too with the front-line commands had disintegrated in several places as Soviet advances swept through at speed. As a result, units collapsed and even became lost or cut off. Consequently, the Soviets knew they had to take advantage of the situation and be quick and decisive. They would have to use overwhelming firepower and huge numbers of soldiers and armored vehicles to prevent the enemy successfully implementing any type of counterstrategy to lengthen the war. All pockets of German resistance would have to be bypassed during the offensive, with certain units later withdrawn from the front to deal with isolated German fortresses. The Soviets were fully aware of Hitler's Fortified Area order and, although this was a hindrance to the smooth running of operations along some parts of the front, overall, the grand Soviet strategy would not be compromised.

Soviet Order of Battle, January–March 1945

2nd Belorussian Front

50th Army (Colonel General Boldin (replaced by Lieutenant General Ozerov)/Major General Garnich)

69th Rifle Corps

81st Rifle Corps

Army Reserve

110th, 153rd Rifle Divisions

307th, 324th Rifle Divisions

343rd Rifle Division

91st, 153rd, 161st Fortified Areas

2nd, 191st Rifle Divisions

49th Army (Lieutenant General Grishin/Major General Kinosyan)

124th Rifle Corps

70th Rifle Corps

121st Rifle Corps

51st, 208th, 216th Rifle Divisions

139th, 238th, 385th Rifle Divisions

42nd, 199th, 380th Rifle Divisions

3rd Army (Lieutenant General Ivashechkin/Colonel General Gorbatov)

40th Rifle Corps

41st Rifle Corps

35th Rifle Corps

3rd Guards Cavalry Corps

5th, 129th, 169th Rifle Divisions

120th Guards, 26th, 283rd Rifle Divisions

250th, 290th, 348th Rifle Divisions

5th, 6th Guards, 32nd Cavalry Divisions

48th Army (Lieutenant General Glebov/Colonel General Gusev)

29th Rifle Corps

53rd Rifle Corps

42nd Rifle Corps

Army Reserve

73rd, 217th Rifle Divisions

17th, 96th, 194th Rifle Divisions

137th, 170th, 399th Rifle Divisions

102nd Rifle Division

2nd Shock Army (Colonel General Fedyuninskii/Lieutenant General Kokorev)

108th Rifle Corps

98th Rifle Corps

116th Rifle Corps

46th, 90th, 372nd Rifle Divisions

142nd, 81st, 381st Rifle Divisions

86th, 321st, 326th Rifle Divisions

65th Army (Colonel General Batov/Lieutenant General Bobkov)

18th Rifle Corps

46th Rifle Corps

105th Rifle Corps

37th Guards, 15th, 69th Rifle Divisions

108th, 186th, 413th Rifle Divisions

44th Guards, 193rd, 354th Rifle Divisions

70th Army (Colonel General Popov/Lieutenant General Lyapin)

96th Rifle Corps

47th Rifle Corps

114th Rifle Corps

38th Guards, 1st, 165th Rifle Divisions

71st, 136th, 162nd Rifle Divisions

76th Guards, 160th, 200th Rifle Divisions

Front Reserve

330th, 369th Rifle Divisions

5th Guards Tank Army (Colonel General of Tank Troops Vol'skii/ Major General of Tank Troops Sidorovich)

10th Tank Corps

29th Tank Corps

47th Independent Mechanized Brigade

1st Guards Motorcycle Regiment

4th Air Army (Colonel General Vershinin/Major General Alekseev)

4th Assault Air Corps

5th Bomber Group

8th Fighter Group

Independent Air Divisions

196th, 199th Assault Air Divisions

132nd, 327th Bomber Divisions

269th, 323rd 215th Fighter Divisions

32nd Assault Air Division

230th, 233rd, 260th Assault Air Divisions

229th, 309th Fighter Divisions,

325th Night Bomber Division

164th Independent Reconnaissance Regiment

Reinforcements

50th Army

144th Artillery Brigade

27th Anti-Tank Artillery Brigade

1321st Anti-Tank Artillery Regiment

181st Mortar Regiment

1484th Anti-Aircraft Artillery Regiment

1444th Self-Propelled Artillery Regiment

50th Engineer-Sapper Brigade

8th Independent Heavy Exploitation Battalion (33rd Assault Engineer Brigade)

49th Army

143rd Artillery Regiment

4th Anti-Tank Artillery Brigade

593rd Anti-Tank Artillery Regiment

540th Independent Mortar Regiment

1273rd Anti-Aircraft Artillery Regiment

544th Independent Mortar Regiment

43rd Anti-Aircraft Artillery Division

7th Guards Tank Regiment

1819th Self-Propelled Artillery Regiment

11th Engineer-Sapper Brigade

48th, 122nd Independent Bridge-Pontoon Battalions

3rd Army

44th Artillery Brigade

2nd Artillery Breakthrough Division

2nd Corps Artillery Brigade

19th Mortar Brigade

44th Anti-Tank Artillery Brigade

584th Independent Anti-Tank Artillery Regiment

475th Independent Mortar Regiment

81st, 56th Howitzer Regiments

517th Corps Artillery Regiment

100th, 77th, 313th Guards Mortar Regiments

1284th Anti-Aircraft Artillery Regiment

28th Anti-Aircraft Artillery Division

Brought from the 49th Army for the artillery preparation:

5 x Rifle Division Artillery Regiments

143rd Artillery Brigade

540th, 544th Independent Mortar Regiments

66th Guards Heavy Tank Regiment

260th Independent Tank Regiment

1812th, 1888th, 1901st, 1294th Self-Propelled Artillery Regiments

340th Guards Heavy Self-Propelled Artillery Regiment

10th Engineer-Sapper Brigade

41st Motorized Engineer Brigade

33rd Independent Exploitation Battalion

179th Independent Bridge Construction Company

48th Army

68th Artillery Brigade

15th Breakthrough Artillery Division (less one battalion from the 106th Heavy Artillery Brigade)

5th, 13th Anti-Tank Artillery Brigades

31st Guards Mortar Brigade

479th Independent Mortar Regiment

461st Anti-Aircraft Artillery Regiment

220th Guards Anti-Tank Artillery Regiment

41st Guards Corps Artillery Regiment

16th Guards Howitzer Regiment

557th Corps Artillery Regiment

6th, 84th Guards Mortar Regiments

286th Mortar Regiment

65th Anti-Aircraft Artillery Regiment

8th Mechanized Corps

23rd Guards Tank Brigade

29th Guards Tank Brigade

342nd Guards Self-Propelled Guards Tank Heavy Artillery Regiment

1902nd, 1199th, 881st Self-Propelled Artillery Regiments

57th Engineer-Sapper Brigade

1st Guards Assault Engineer-Sapper Brigade

34th Independent Flamethrower Company

2nd Shock Army

81st Artillery Brigade

8th Breakthrough Artillery Corps (23rd, 1st Artillery Divisions)

4th, 7th Guards Mortar Brigades

138th, 1099th Corps Artillery Regiments

89th 43rd Guards Mortar Regiments

47th Anti-Aircraft Artillery Division

760th Independent Anti-Tank Artillery Regiment

230th Guards Mortar Regiment

803rd Anti-Aircraft Artillery Regiment

8th Guards Tank Corps

30th Guards Heavy Tank Brigade

46th Guards Heavy Tank Regiment

1196th, 1294th, 1476th, 1434th Self-Propelled Artillery Regiments

21st Engineer-Sapper Brigade

3rd Assault Engineer-Sapper Brigade

65th Army

147th Artillery Brigade

3rd Breakthrough Artillery Corps (26th, 18th Artillery Divisions)

1st Anti-Tank Artillery Brigade

5th Guards Mortar Brigade

143rd Guards Mortar Regiment

543rd Anti-Tank Artillery Regiment

235th Anti-Aircraft Regiment

49th Howitzer Regiment

85th Guards Howitzer Regiment

18th, 62nd Guards Mortar Regiments

12th Anti-Aircraft Division

1st Guards Tank Corps

80th Guards Tank Regiment

251st Independent Tank Regiment

510th Independent Tank Flamethrower Regiment

40th Independent Engineer Tank Regiment

985th, 922nd, 1495th, 999th Self-Propelled Artillery Regiments

14th Engineer-Sapper Brigade

1st Assault Engineer-Sapper Brigade

36th Independent Flamethrower Company

70th Army

148th Artillery Brigade

378th Anti-Tank Artillery Regiment

136th Guards Mortar Regiment

581st Anti-Aircraft Artillery Regiment

317th Heavy Caliber Battalion

325th Guards Mortar Regiment

74th Anti-Aircraft Division (expected from the Leningrad Front)

1898th, 1890th Self-Propelled Artillery Regiments

85th, 133rd, 259th Independent Self-Propelled Artillery Battalions

48th Engineer-Sapper Brigade

7th Pontoon-Bridge Regiment

9th, 87th, 42nd, 89th Independent Motorized Pontoon-Bridge Battalions

Reserve Front

13th Guards Mortar Brigade

15th, 19th Anti-Tank Artillery Brigades

1268th, 1270th, 1479th, 341st, 1709th, 1482nd, 225th, 739th Independent Anti-Aircraft Artillery Regiments

21st, 14th, 490th, 614th, 451st, 508th Independent Anti-Aircraft Artillery Battalions (High Command Reserve)

3rd Guards Tank Corps

233rd Independent Tank Regiment

1023rd Self-Propelled Artillery Regiment

36th, 104th Motorized Pontoon-Bridge Battalions

8th Independent Exploitation Tank Battalion

49th Independent Exploitation Tank Company

141st Independent Motorized Signals Company

4th Pontoon-Bridge Brigade

5th Pontoon-Bridge Regiment

72nd Guards Motorized-Engineer Battalion

33rd Motorized Engineer-Minesweeper Bridge Brigade

77th Independent Bridge Construction Battalion

3rd Independent Flamethrower Company

11th Independent Engineer-Minesweeper Regiment

5th Guards Tank Army

4th Air Corps

201st Light Artillery Brigade

689th Independent Anti-Tank Artillery Regiment

6th Anti-Tank Artillery Regiment

14th Guards Independent Tank Regiment

376th Guards Heavy Self-Propelled Artillery Regiment

21st Motorized Engineer Regiment

In Profile:
SU-122 Self-Propelled Gun, 1st Guards Tank Army and T-34-85 Tank, 5th Guards Tank Army, February 1945

This SU-122 self-propelled gun has been painted in a sand base color with mottled-green patches sprayed over the vehicle body. The SU-122 proved effective in its intended role of direct fire on strongholds and was very successful against heavy German armor in East Pomerania. (Oliver Missing)

This T-34-85 once received a coating of winter whitewash which has now faded, revealing the original summer-green camouflage spray. The T-34-85 took part in all engagements on the battlefield and successfully encountered a mix of late Panzer IVs (Ausf.G, H, and J), Panthers, Tigers, and many tank-hunters. (Oliver Missing)

Soviet Commanders

2nd Belorussian Front

General Konstantin Konstantinovich Rokossovsky (December 21, 1896–August 3, 1968)

Rokossovsky always said that he was Polish, and though he lived in Russia until the end of his life, he spoke Russian with a strong Polish accent. In Poland, he is remembered mainly for the fact that he commanded the famous 1st and then the 2nd Belorussian Fronts which brought about so many victories. Rokossovsky was a brilliant tactician and a master of offensive operations. Out in the field he had the ability to recognize the enemy's intentions and use their weaknesses to his advantage. He could often be seen in the trenches at the front among his men. "If a long time passes without going to the trenches," he said, "there is a feeling as if some important link has been broken, and some very valuable information has been lost." In the summer of 1944, he confirmed his status as a great commander during Operation *Bagration*, the liberation of Belorussia. Rokossovsky was awarded the Diamond Star of the Soviet Union Marshal for his part in *Bagration*. In November 1944, he was transferred to the 2nd Belorussian Front, which had advanced into East Prussia. From East Prussia, in February 1945, Rokossovsky was ordered to prepare for the offensive operation in East Pomerania to clear out German positions and cover the right flank of a Soviet advance on Berlin.

1st and 2nd Belorussian Fronts

Although Zhukov did not play a major role in the East Pomeranian offensive, the success of operations in Pomerania allowed Zhukov's forces of the 1st Belorussian Front to advance to the Oder in preparation for the battle of Berlin. There had been much speculation about who would lead the army to the gates of the Nazi capital. In his memoirs, Rokossovsky recalled a telephone conversation he'd had with Stalin: "It was so unexpected that, in the heat of the moment, I immediately asked: 'Why this disfavor of being moved from the main area of operations to a secondary sector?' Stalin replied that I was mistaken: The sector to which I was being transferred was part of the overall western area of operations, in which the forces of three fronts would be operating—the 2nd Belorussian, 1st Belorussian, and 1st Ukrainian Front—and the success of this decisive operation will be dependent on the close coordination of these fronts. 'If you and Konev fail to advance, Zhukov will not advance either,' the Supreme Commander-in-chief said in conclusion." However, it

Commanders Marshal Konstantin Rokossovsky (left) and Marshal Georgy Zhukov conversing.

was believed by Rokossovsky that Stalin had already made up his mind that Zhukov would take Berlin. Instead, his 2nd Belorussian Front would destroy enemy formations in East Prussia and East Pomerania and prevent the powerful German Third Panzer Army from taking part in the battle of Berlin.

1st Guard Tank Army

Marshal of Tank Troops Mikhail Katukov (September 17, 1900–June 8, 1976)

Katukov led his tank troops during the Konitz–Koslin offensive during the opening phase of the East Pomeranian operations. His army went on to take part in the Vistula–Oder operation, and then in the battle of Berlin.

Grishin studying a map.

49th Army

Lieutenant General Ivan Grishin (December 16, 1901–June 20, 1951)

From February 10, 1945, Grishin's 49th Army was ordered to take part in the East Pomeranian offensive. On February 21, he captured Czersk and on March 10 he was promoted to colonel general. Three weeks later, on March 30, his army captured the fortified city of Danzig along with the 2nd Shock, 65th, and 70th Armies.

50th Army

Colonel General Ivan Boldin (August 3, 1892–March 28, 1965)

Boldin remained continuously in command of the 50th Army on the Eastern Front until February 1945. The army did not participate in the East Pomeranian offensive, except for mopping up and securing the flanks of the main spearhead. Boldin was relieved of his command and the 50th Army was transferred to the 3rd Belorussian Front.

65th Army

Colonel General Pavel Batov (June 1, 1897–April 19, 1985)

Batov took command of the 65th Army in late 1942. Rokossovsky later wrote about Batov's leadership skills: "[He] displayed fine initiative with an improvised mobile task force … By striking at the enemy's flank and rear, the task force ensured the swift advance of the other units." The army took part in the Altdamm offensive operation in March 1945. It was also committed to the Danzig offensive, along with the 2nd Shock Army, 49th Army, and 19th Army.

70th Army

General Vasily Popov (January 8, 1894–July 2, 1967)

From February to March 1945 Popov's army took part in the East Pomeranian offensive and assisted in the capture of Danzig in March. During the Stettin–Rostock operation, the 70th Army operated as part of the 2nd Belorussian Front towards Neubrandenburg. After crossing the Oder, the German Stettin Group was defeated. Popov reached the city of Rostock and the Baltic Coast near Wismar on May 3.

2nd Guards Tank Army

General Semyon Ilyich Bogdanov (September 10, 1894–March 12, 1960)

From September 1944, Bogdanov was given the command of the 2nd Guards Tank Army. In February 1945 his army took part in the Konitz–Koslin offensive, and in March the Danzig offensive operation. For his leadership, Bogdanov was awarded the title Hero of the Soviet Union on March 11, 1945.

3rd Shock Army

General Nikolai Pavlovich Simoniak (February 17, 1901–April 19, 1955)

In October 1944 Simoniak was appointed commander of the 3rd Shock Army, which fought in the blockade of the Kurland Pocket, the Warsaw–Poznan offensive, and the East Pomeranian offensive. On March 16, 1945, he was replaced by General Vasily Kuznetso.

2nd Shock Army

Colonel General Ivan Fedyuninsky (July 30, 1900–October 17, 1977)

In December 1943, Fedyuninsky was appointed commander of the 2nd Shock Army. A year later he led his army against German Army Group North in operations around Kurland, East Prussia, and East Pomerania. For operations in East Pomerania, the 2nd Shock Army reinforced the left flank of the 2nd Belorussian Front for the offensive along the western bank of the Vistula River, to arrive as quickly as possible at the Bay of Danzig. Fedyuninsky was heavily embroiled in the Danzig offensive operation and clearing German defenses in Pomerania.

Fedyuninsky in 1939, as a lieutenant colonel.

In Profile:
T-34-85 Tank and IS-2 Heavy Tank, 8th Guards Tank Corps, 2nd Shock Army, Danzig, March 1945

A T-34-85 tank with its whitewash covering the dark-green summer camouflage paint which is still evident. (Oliver Missing)

An IS-2 from the 1196th Heavy Tank Regiment with whitewash covering the olive-green summer camouflage paint. These tanks supported infantry in the assault by destroying bunkers, buildings, and dug-in weapons, and engaging enemy armored vehicles. They were very effective in urbanized combat. (Oliver Missing)

Preparations for Pomerania

In order to clear the northern parts of the Eastern Front following the successful Soviet spearheads through the Baltic states, the Soviet 2nd Belorussian Front had initially planned on sending its powerful formations west and north of the River Vistula toward Pomerania and the major seaport of Danzig. Its main objective was to protect the right flank of the 1st Belorussian Front, which was advancing at speed to the Oder River.

During the East Prussian offensive, or what was known to the Soviets as Operation *Goldap–Gumbinnen*, the 2nd Belorussian Front had been ordered in January 1945 to drive north toward Elbing between Braunsberg and Heiligenbeil. However, the front had been severely weakened by continual fighting and as result received one hundred and twenty thousand replacement personnel, but none from the Soviet home reinforcement organization. Just shy of forty thousand of the replacements were wounded or sick who were returned to duty. Some twenty thousand others were pulled from the rear echelons, which included supply services. Another ten thousand were former Soviet prisoners who had been liberated from German POW camps, and fifty-three thousand were fresh conscripts, primarily from the recaptured areas of Poland, Ukraine, and the Baltic states. The bulk of these men, however, had been forced into the Red Army with little or no training and were up against well-seasoned, experienced enemy soldiers. The Soviets though used heavy firepower and overwhelming numbers of soldiers to systematically grind down their enemy.

When the initial phase of the East Prussian offensive was finally over, it left a large number of German forces intact in Pomerania, where they threatened the right flank of Zhukov's formations advancing on the Oder to attack Berlin. As a result, the 2nd Belorussian Front was redeployed from East Prussia to attack westward into Pomerania. The attack would open a new offensive, known as the East Pomeranian offensive. Its sole objective was to clear and destroy German formations in Pomerania and secure the flanks to protect the 1st Belorussian Front undertaking its final drive on Berlin. The offensive would run simultaneously with the Soviet Silesian offensive of General Konev's 1st Ukrainian Front. Both offensives were designed to protect the Soviet attack on the Reich capital.

Initially the East Pomeranian offensive was planned for early February 1945. However, there were delays with Soviet generals arguing over who was capable of capturing Berlin the fastest and with the fewest casualties. There was also concern among the Soviet planners that undefeated German formations should not remain on the flanks of the Red Army spearheads, as these might mount a surprise counterattack and prolong the war. For this reason, Soviet forces of the 2nd Belorussian Front would be moved from East Prussia to East Pomerania.

In Profile:
Soviet M1943 120mm Mortar Crew and PPSh-41 Submachine Gunner in Action, Danzig, March 1945

A Soviet mortar crew in action against enemy positions in Danzig, March 1945. This muzzle-loading mortar was easily broken down into three parts—barrel, bipod, and base plate—for movement over short distances, or towed by a GAZ-66 truck on a two-wheel tubular carriage.

A Soviet submachine gunner uses a demolished building as cover during street fighting in Danzig. He is armed with his "Papasha" PPSh-41 submachine gun. He wears the *ushanka* winter fur cap and the standard infantryman's coat with black leather belt and high black boots.

However, as plans were put into place to redeploy the 2nd Belorussian Front to prepare for its new offensive operation in East Pomerania, on February 15, 1945, the Germans mounted a surprise counterattack from Stargard in Pomerania to relieve the city of Kustrin, known as Operation *Solstice*. The plan was in direct response, as predicted by the Soviets, to the Red Army advance on Berlin. Surprisingly, the German Eleventh SS Panzer Army, which by February 5 had been subordinated to Army Group Vistula, was able to pull together over one thousand two hundred tanks to the offensive. This was one of the most powerful armies that the Germans had left in their arsenal on the Eastern Front. It comprised an ad hoc Tettau Corps Group, the X SS Corps, and the III Germanic SS Panzer Corps, comprising volunteers from the Nederland, Nordland, and Langemarck divisions. It was also supported by the XXXIX Panzer Corps, Panzer Division Holstein, and the 9th Fallschirmjäger Division.

The attack by the 11th SS opened successfully by pushing Red Army formations back some six miles and reoccupying territory on the eastern shore of Lake Madu, as well as by recapturing Pyritz. Large numbers of Soviet antitank guns and tanks were destroyed by Tiger II tanks, but these heavy German panzers also took heavy losses. The German attacks and increased air activity compounded Soviet difficulties; Soviet units faced supply bottlenecks, resulting in urgent requests for antiaircraft weapons. Yet, despite an audacious start by the Germans, much of the progress was hindered by unrelenting Soviet resistance and massed artillery support. To blunt the attack, Zhukov threw the 3rd Shock Army into the battle, which had redeployed from Jastrow. The German offensive stalled. Army Group Vistula halted on the *Sonnenwende*, the Solstice, on February 18. Days later, Zhukov deployed the 61st and the 2nd Guards Tank Armies, including the 7th Guards Cavalry Corps, to capture Stettin. What followed was bitter fighting with house-to-house combat in the rubble-strewn streets of Arnswalde. Initially, the Germans stubbornly held their positions, but within days, to avoid complete destruction, German commanders evacuated their decimated formations from the heavy fighting. The withdrawal also included moving the XXXIX Panzer Corps headquarters, as well as the Führer-Grenadier, Führer-Begleit, Holstein, and 10th SS Panzer Divisions, west behind Army Group Center. As a result, the German counterattack was a failure, but the operation did convince the Soviets to postpone their attack on Berlin while its forces took up positions ready to clear East Pomerania.

With the German counterattack in tatters, East Pomerania was now vulnerable more than ever to a major Soviet counterattack. For this reason, Hitler denied further freedom of movement, deducing that the Red Army was preparing its own plan for a counterattack in Pomerania before its main forces advanced on Berlin. Army Group Vistula, comprising the Second Army, was totally exposed throughout Pomerania and running east to the borders of East Prussia at Elbing. General Weiß requested permission to withdraw from the area, but Hitler refused. His troops would have to dig in and defend. With withdrawal refused, the bulk of the Second Army were doomed. By February 18 the city of Grudenz, on the Vistula, was surrounded; the garrison of the German 83rd Infantry Division were ordered to defend the city to the bloody end, as can be seen in the following report taken from *Prelude to Berlin: The Red Army's Offensive Operations in Poland and Eastern Germany, 1945* and which was made by the Soviet General Staff:

> Report by the Commander of the Second Belorussian Front No. 3708. To the Chief of the General Staff on the Plan for Employing the 19th Army and the 3rd Guards Tank Corps.

15 February 1945

I report:

1. According to Stavka of the Supreme High Command directive No. 11021 of 8.02.1945, the front has been entrusted with the objective of no later than 20.02.1945 of reaching the line at the mouth of the Vistula River–Dirschau–Berent–Rummelsberg–Neustettin. Subsequently, upon the arrival of the 19th Army, we are to develop the offensive in the general direction of Stettin, capturing the Danzig–Gdynia area, and clearing the coastline of the enemy as far as the Bay of Pomerania.

2. Taking into account the front's available forces, I believe that it is more expedient to employ the 19th Army and the 3rd Guards Tank Corps along the front's left wing, with the objective, deploying along the line Schlochau–Ratzebor, to attack in the general direction of Baldenburg, Bublitz and Kezlin, for the purpose of splitting up the enemy's Pomeranian group of forces and arriving at the shore of the Baltic Sea along the front of the Jamundersee–Kolberg. The elimination of the enemy east of the Konitz–Rugenwalde meridian will be entrusted to the front's right-flank forces, consisting of the 2nd Shock, 65th, 49th, and 70th armies.

3. The beginning of the commitment of the 19th Army and 3rd Guards Tank Corps into the fighting is possible only from 22–23 February, as it is necessary to carry out a 160-kilometer march to the deployment line. The beginning of the movement is from 17.02.1945.

4. In order to carry out the Stavka of the Supreme High Command's assignment on clearing the enemy out of Pomerania and reaching the Bay of Pomerania, the following are necessary:

a) to reinforce the front's left wing with two combined-arms armies and two tank corps. Moreover, it is necessary to carry this out upon the arrival of the 19th Army and the 3rd Guards Tank Corps in the Neustettin area, for with the movement of these forces to the northeast it will be necessary to secure the Kezlin axis from the west;

b) the front's right-wing armies, which have been involved in intensive fighting for the past month, have suffered heavy casualties and are now under strength, amounting to, on the average, 26 3,000-man and eight 4,000-man rifle divisions. In order to bring these divisions at least up to 6,000 men, we need a centrally trained reinforcement of up to 80,000 men, and up to 20,000 men for reinforcing the specialized combat arms.

Rokossovskii

Subbotin

Kotov

Directive of the Stavka of the VGK No. 11026. To the Commander of the Second Belorussian Front on the Confirmation of the Plan to Employ the 19th Army and the 3rd Guards Tank Corps (via *Prelude to Berlin*):

17 February 1945, 2010 hrs The Stavka of the Supreme High Command orders:

The 19th Army and the 3rd Guards Tank Corps are to be employed in accordance with plan No. 3708, of 15.02.45 which you presented.

2. Establish from 2400 20.02.1945 the following boundary line between the Second and First Belorussian fronts: Bromberg–Flederborn–Neustettin–Kolberg (all locales for the First Belorussian Front).

3. For your information, on 19.02.1945 the First Belorussian Front's right-wing forces will attack along the Falkenberg and Gollnow axes.

4. Report on orders issued.

Stavka of the Supreme High Command

I. Stalin

A. Vasilevskii

Directive of the Stavka VGK No. 11033. To the Commanders of the Third and Second Belorussian Fronts on the Elaboration of Their Objectives and the Change in Their Boundary Line (via *Prelude to Berlin*):

21 February 1945, 2200 hrs

The Stavka of the Supreme High Command orders:

To establish from 2400 24.02.1945 the following boundary line between the Second and Third Belorussian fronts: as far as Osterode as before, then Saalfeld–Christburg–Halbstadt (on the Nogat River)–Nickelswalde (all locales for the Third Belorussian Front). The commander of the Third Belorussian Front is to be ready by this date to relieve the forces of the Second Belorussian Front within the new boundary lines. The responsibility for securing the boundary between the fronts remains with the commander of the Third Belorussian Front.

2. The commander of the Second Belorussian Front is to employ the freed-up forces of the 2nd Shock Army to reinforce the army's left flank for an offensive along the western bank of the Vistula River, for the purpose of arriving as quickly as possible at the shore of the Bay of Danzig.

3. The commander of the Third Belorussian Front is to more quickly move his left wing to the shore of the Bay of Danzig east of the Vistula River, for the purpose of closing the exit from the Frische-Nehrung spit.

4. Report on orders issued.

Stavka of the Supreme High Command

I. Stalin

A. Antonov

The Stavka (via *Prelude to Berlin*) highlighted the following for the conduct of operations in East Pomerania:

Area of Combat Operations and the Germans' Defensive Structures

The area of combat operations embraces East Pomerania in the following boundaries: in the north, the shore of the Baltic Sea from Bosniak at the mouth of the Vistula River, as far as the Diwenow Strait; in the east, as far as the Vistula River from Bosniak to Bydgoszcz (Bromberg); in the south, the Bydgoszcz Canal and the Netze and Warta rivers as far as Küstrin, and; in the west, the Oder River. The Second Belorussian Front's area of combat operations includes the eastern part of Pomerania to the east of the line Kolberg–Polzyn–Schneidemühl as far as

In Profile: T-34-85 Tank and BM-13N "Katyusha" Rocket Launcher, Kolberg, March 1945

This 1st Guards Tank Army (31st Tank Corps) T-34-85 tank, temporarily assigned from the 1st to the 2nd Belorussian Front for operations against Kolberg, has received a full coating of winter whitewash. (Oliver Missing)

The "Katyusha." These multiple-rocket launchers were often found in independent rocket batteries supporting armored, infantry and artillery assaults. This one is supporting the 11th Guards Tank Corps, 1st Belorussian Front. Almost half of the rocket batteries were equipped with the BM-13 type of launcher. This particular one, set up upon the chassis of the Soviet Zi6-6 six-wheeled utility truck, has been modified to include a 16-rocket launch system. It has received a very light whitewash coating over its olive-green summer camouflage paint. (Oliver Missing)

the port of Danzig and the Vistula River. The overall size of the area is twenty-two thousand five hundred square miles.

A Description of the Area's Surface

The area under study is a hilly plain, thirty to thirty-five percent of which is covered by coniferous and leafy woods. The area is bordered from the south to the shore of the Baltic Sea by the area of the Baltic uplands, consisting of a large number of small hills and ridges, covered by boulders, sands, and loamy soil. The area of the Baltic uplands is distinguished by the Kaszub uplands, which stretch from the towns of Danzig and Gdynia to the west as far as the Stolp River, and the Pomeranian uplands, which stretch from the line of the Stolp River southwest to the Oder River. The Kaszub uplands are the highest and most broken part of the entire zone of the Baltic uplands. The predominant absolute heights are one hundred to two hundred meters. The highest point in this area is Mount Tumberg, 331 meters above sea level. The area's relief is hilly; the relative height of the hilly ridges is fifty to seventy meters. The steepness of the slopes is upwards of fifteen to twenty degrees. Between the hills is a multiplicity of lakes, predominantly of elongated form, with narrow defiles between the lakes. In a number of places, chains of lakes stretching from north to south in several rows form a series of natural obstacles. The Pomeranian uplands are a hilly plain, stretching two hundred kilometers in length toward the southwest from the Kaszub uplands. The dominant heights are one hundred and fifty to two hundred meters. The Pomeranian uplands are less broken and are distinguished by a softer relief, although the presence of a large number of lakes with narrow defiles between them impedes the maneuver by tank and mechanized forces. The soil found in the area of the eastern part of Pomerania along the coast is sandy and of clay in the middle and southern parts of the area. The presence of clay soil in the greater part of the area makes movement off the roads difficult in the spring and fall.

The Area's Hydrography

There are a large number of rivers and lakes in East Pomerania. The Vistula River flows along the area's eastern boundary. The Vistula River is navigable by ships along its entire course within the area's boundaries. The river's width along various sectors reaches one thousand five hundred to one thousand eight hundred meters, while its depth varies from 1.5–6 meters, and there are no fords. The speed of the current is 0.5–1.5 meters per second. The Vistula River is a powerful water line covering East Pomerania from the east. Along the area's southern boundary, as if covering the approach to East Prussia from the south, are the Netze and Warta rivers, connected with the Vistula River by the Bydgoszcz Canal. The canal is forty kilometers long, fifteen to twenty meters wide and 1.5–3 meters deep. The Netze River is three hundred and twenty kilometers long, twenty to fifty meters wide, one to three meters deep, and has a speed of 0.5–0.7 meters per second. The Netze River has a broad flood plain, which in some sectors reaches twelve to fifteen kilometers. This creates certain difficulties in overcoming it. Along the sector from Santok to Küstrin, along the southern part of the area, flows the Warta River on its lower course. The width of the Warta River in this area is about one hundred meters. The Oder River flows along the area's western boundary. The Stolp, Wipper, Persante, and Rega rivers flow into the Baltic Sea, in the northern part of East Pomerania. None of the rivers, either those in the northern or the southern parts of East Pomerania, are major water barriers; they may be overcome at any

In Profile: Grenadier with Sturmgewehr 44 and a *Volkssturm* Panzerschreck Fighter

A grenadier armed with the famous StG 44 assault rifle during a reconnaissance operation in early April 1944. He is holding the Dienstglas 6×30 field binoculars. Tucked in his black leather infantryman's belt is a Stielhandgranate 24 stick grenade. Attached to his belt is the StG 44 ammunition pouch. (Renato Dalmaso)

This *Volkssturm* (Home Guard) fighter is armed with the Panzerschreck ("tank fright"), the popular name for the Raketenpanzerbüchse 54 (Rocket Anti-armor Rifle Model 54, abbreviated to RPzB 54), an 8.8cm reusable antitank launcher. (Renato Dalmaso)

time of the year by forces without special training. The exception is the February–March period, during the spring runoff, when the water rises 1–1.5 meters above its usual level. To the north, East Pomerania is washed by the waters of the Baltic Sea. Along the entire territory of East Pomerania there is a large number of large and small lakes. The southwestern part of East Pomerania is particularly rich in lakes. Up to two hundred and fifty lakes, large and small, are scattered to the southwest of the line Schneidemühl–Polzyn. There are also a significant number of lakes to the northeast of the line Schneidemühl–Polzyn. Lakes, rivers, and the canals connecting them restrict troop movements during an offensive and favor the creation of a solid defense.

Communications Lines

East Pomerania has a broadly developed road network. The railroads are primarily two-tracked. The overall railroad density is sufficiently high and reaches 10.5 kilometers per 100 square miles of territory. The average density of the paved and dirt roads in the area is 30.5 kilometers per 100 square miles. The majority of its paved roads have a gravel and tar surface. The surface of all country and improved roads is stones or bricks. The Chojnice–Stettin highway passes through the area, with branches to Küstrin. The main water arteries in the area are the Vistula, Netze, Warta, Oder, and Brae rivers, and the Bydgoszcz Canal.

Seaports

From the north the shores of the eastern Pomeranian area are washed by the Baltic Sea for a distance of two hundred and fifty kilometers. Here are located major seaports, which are bases for the Germans' surface and submarine fleets. The port of Danzig is well outfitted as a commercial port, and is of international significance. The port of Gdynia (Gotenhaven) has been transformed into a major naval base for the German navy, where submarines and surfaces ships of all classes are based and repaired. Besides this, there are a number of small ports along the coast of the Baltic Sea: Stolpmünde, Rugenwaldermunde, and Kolberg. These ports are the best places for making naval landings.

Communications

The territory of East Pomerania was fitted out with a sufficiently dense communications network. All towns and the overwhelming majority of inhabited locales in rural areas were linked by a telephone–telegraph network, which made it easier to organize communications and troop control. The presence of a network of underground communications lines and a large number of bypass lines, despite the Germans having destroyed a certain amount of them while retreating, guaranteed that the Second Belorussian Front's attacking forces had reliable communications.

The *Volkssturm* was established in October 1944 as a militia utilizing males between the ages of 16 and 60 who were not otherwise serving in the Wehrmacht or other military units. They were under the control of the Nazi party and its officials (Gauleiters), with Heinrich Himmler as commander.

Konitz–Koslin Offensive, February 24–March 6, 1945

The Red Army looked upon their winter offensive in January 1945 as the last great push on the Eastern Front. The principal objective was to crush the remaining German forces in Poland, East Prussia, and the Baltic states. Along the Baltic, an all-out Soviet assault began in earnest with the main intention of crushing the remaining understrength German units of the once-vaunted Army Group North, while the German defenders attempted to stall the massive Red Army push with the weapons and men remaining at their disposal.

The Soviet 3rd Belorussian Front launched its westwards assault toward the ancient Prussian city of Königsberg against strong defensive positions of the Third Panzer Army and Fourth Army. To support the 3rd Belorussian Front, General Rokossovsky's 2nd Belorussian Front was ordered on January 20 to swing north from the River Narew toward the town of Elbing. The 2nd Belorussian Front would play a pivotal part in the fighting, especially in East Pomerania. As Rokossovsky's infantry and tanks advanced, they caught the Third

Whitewashed Pz.Kpfw. IVs advance across the snowy steppe.

A commander of a whitewashed StuG 40 Ausf.G greets a member of the Gebirgsjäger. The XVIII Mountain Corps was placed under the Second Army during the offensive.

Panzer Army and Fourth Army by surprise. On the 2nd Belorussian's right flank, the 3rd Guards Cavalry Corps captured the town of Allenstein on 22 January, threatening rear units of the Fourth Army. Four days later, advanced elements of the 2nd Belorussian Front reached the coast at the Vistula Lagoon, severing land communications with the entire Fourth Army and several divisions of the Second Army, which was now encircled in what became known as the Heiligenbeil Pocket/Cauldron/*Kessel*. As Red Army troops compressed the pocket, fighting intensified as German soldiers feverishly tried to escape with their lives.

A heavy mountain gun troop prepares to move during offensive operations in the snow. Note the MG-34 machine gun on its tripod mount on the sled. (Lafette 34)

Commander of the 2nd Belorussian Front Marshal Rokossovsky (second from left), with Military Council member A. A. Lobachev and the writer Stavsky inspecting captured enemy equipment following a German withdrawal from the area.

Red Army Order of Battle

2nd Belorussian Front (Marshal Konstantin Rokossovsky)

1st Belorussian Front (eastern flank) (Marshal Georgy Zhukov)

3rd Shock Army

1st Guards Tank Army

2nd Guards Tank Army

A commander of the 8th Guards Tank Corps, 2nd Shock Army, 2nd Belorussian Front, addresses his tank troops prior to battle, on February 23, 1945.

Wehrmacht Order of Battle

Army Group Vistula

Second Army (General Walter Weiß)

XXXXVI Panzer Corps

XXVII Panzer Corps

XXIII Corps

XVIII Mountain Corps

Fortress Garrisons of Graudenz and Danzig

Third Panzer Army (re-formed) (eastern flank) (General Erhard Raus)

III SS Panzer Corps

X SS Corps

An old whitewashed 15cm Nebelwerfer 41 rocket launcher being prepared for a fire mission in the snow by a unit of *Nebeltruppen*. This weapon was fired from a six-tube launcher mounted on a towed carriage adapted from that used by the 3.7cm Pak 36.

Winter-clad German soldiers. Note how their two-piece winter reversibles, white-side-out, have become soiled with dirt and grime. This discoloration often made concealment in the snow more difficult.

Winter-clad grenadiers at a forward observation post during a reconnaissance mission.

A knocked-out Soviet T-34 tank in front of a dead horse and a destroyed wagon.

With German forces either encircled or setting up defensive positions in and around villages and towns, Rokossovsky was ordered to clear enemy-occupied East Pomerania. A plan known as the East Pomeranian offensive had been drawn up. The first phase of the plan was known as the Konitz–Koslin offensive operation. In total there would be four phases of the offensive to ensure the German forces were effectively driven out or destroyed in East Pomerania, so that there would be no further threats of an enemy counterattack to prevent the final push on Berlin.

Following the failed German counterattack, German intelligence sent out a warning of the danger of a large-scale Soviet offensive. Plans were immediately drawn up and sent to front-line commands; these plans stated that the troops should improve their present positions and stand fast and fight. The order also included Hitler's *Fester Platz*, where fortified areas were to be immediately established in several main towns and cities and manned by fanatical German units to stem the Red Army onslaught. Several locales had already been fortified and turned into fortresses, such as Arnswalde, Altdamn, Breslau, Danzig, Stettin, Koslin, Kustrin, Kolberg, Folburg, Insterburg, and Königsberg.

Along the German front, soldiers were slowly becoming aware of the imminent danger of an attack. By February 22, 1945, German intelligence was monitoring increased enemy activity along the front. German defenses varied considerably, and were organized in special defensive regions and belts, antitank strongpoints, and a crude network of engineer obstacles. The defenses varied along the whole front, from robust concrete gun emplacements supported by Pak or Flak guns to a series of foxholes and slit trenches, manned by a host of heavy and light MG-34 or MG-42 machine guns, as well as the 7.5cm and 8.8cm Paks. However, due to supply issues, ammunition was at a premium, and many of the weapons could not sustain a defense for any appreciable length of time. Even the average German

Grenadiers during defensive operations in late February 1945. Note the officer armed with a StG 44 or Sturmgewehr 44 assault rifle.

Heer troops wearing their distinctive splinter camo smocks during operations in 1945. These troops are more than likely on a reconnaissance mission to deduce the location and movement of the enemy.

Soviet T-34 tanks drive across the snow during the first phase of the East Pomeranian offensive in late February 1945. Note the troops clinging to the side of the tank hull. At a moment's notice the soldiers will quickly dismount and charge into action.

Grenadiers moving quickly during defensive fighting in late February 1945. Note the soldier armed with the lethal Panzerfaust.

Volkssturm troops armed with a light MG-34 in action.

soldier knew the German position was overstretched and lacked the proper manpower or reserves to be properly defensible. The lack of armored support, too, was another serious concern for field commanders, who were under no illusions as to the gargantuan task ahead.

The Soviet offensive finally opened on February 24 with the newly drafted troops of Kozlov's 19th Army. Supporting the attack were thousands of guns and mortars, including Katyusha multiple-rocket launchers which poured fire and destruction onto the German front. The opening bombardment was so heavy in some sectors along the German front that soldiers, fearing complete annihilation, deserted their trenches and foxholes to save themselves from

A Sturmgeschütz III advancing through a village.

A tank unit belonging to the 2nd Belorussian Front advances along a forest road into East Pomerania. On February 27 elements of the 2nd Belorussian Front entered Pomerania, and the next day they captured Neustettin.

A still from a German newsreel depicting German troops on the march in Pomerania. To the left is a Sturmgeschütz III.

Volkssturm troops in Pomerania preparing the defense.

A column of Soviet self-propelled SU-76Ms on a road in northern Pomerania, March 1945. The SU-76M virtually replaced light tanks in the close-support role during the later part of the war. While its thin armor and open top made it vulnerable to antitank weapons and grenades, its light weight and low silhouette gave it good maneuverability.

the rain of fire. Several Red Army reconnaissance assaults were made successfully, but after twelve miles of breakthrough, the attack was suddenly halted by intense German resistance. Soviet artillery devoted time to pulverizing the German defensive positions and destroying areas deep behind German lines, but for two days the German lines held.

On February 26, the 3rd Guards Tank Corps was deployed east of Neustettin, where it achieved several successful breakthroughs at Baldenburg. Fighting in and around Neustettin continued to rage at great cost until it was finally captured by the left flank of the 3rd Guards Cavalry Corps on February 27.

Whilst the Red Army continued to attack, the VII Panzer Corps was hastily assembled to assist with defensive measures. It was comprised of the Panzergrenadier Division Grossdeutschland, 24th Panzer Division, 299th Infantry Division, 18th Panzergrenadier

A T-34-85 tank with infantry riders advances along an East Pomeranian road bound for the front. Note part of a track link has been bolted to the side of the turret to provide additional protection against antitank rounds.

Winter-clad grenadiers have hitched a lift on a column of Sturmgeschütz IIIs. On the edge of the battlefield these troops would dismount and go into action.

Division, 23rd Infantry Division, and remnants of the 7th Panzer Division. The VII Panzer Corps came under the German Second Army and was comprised of a motley assortment of self-propelled vehicles, Sturmgeschütz III/IVs, Tigers, Panthers, Pz.Kpf. IVs, and Hezters. These panzer units with supporting panzergrenadier *truppen* were deployed to the town of Rummelsburg to attack advancing Red Army units of the 19th Army. Simultaneously, as fighting raged in and around Rummelsburg, Soviet units advanced on Konitz with the main objective of capturing Koslin, using special assault groups trained and equipped to

A whitewashed Sturmgeschütz III with winter-clad infantry on board passes a burning Soviet vehicle.

A Soviet mortar crew with their 120mm mortar prepare to fire. The firepower of this mortar was impressive. These weapons were commonly found in Soviet rifle divisions which boasted 12 of these fearsome weapons, giving the Soviet rifle regiments an edge over their German counterparts.

smash through defensive positions. For two days Soviet troops attacked toward Koslin, but the Germans were determined to hold their positions at all costs and repelled the attackers using a variety of heavy and light artillery pieces supported by assault guns and groups

A battery of BM-13 Katyusha multiple-rocket launchers opens fire. By March 1945, some 518 batteries were in Red Army service.

Using a bombed-out building for concealment, a young Red Army artillery crew prepare their 76mm M1942 (ZiS-3) divisional gun.

A staged photograph showing a Soviet unit street-fighting inside a town (which has probably already been captured). The solders are armed with the PPS-43 submachine gun.

A German Panzerschrek team preparing their weapon for action. This Raketenpanzerbüchse 54 (Rocket Anti-armor Rifle Model 54, abbreviated to RPzB 54) was an 8.8cm reusable antitank rocket launcher, nicknamed "*Ofenrohr*" or stovepipe.

armed with Panzerfaust rocket grenades. In the town of Konitz, a German garrison was formed; the soldiers there were ordered to defend it to the last man. Fighting in and around the town was a fierce contest of attrition, and although the Germans showed great fortitude

A T34-85 from General Bogdanov 2nd Guards Tank Army advancing through a town. In February 1945 the 2nd Guards Tank Army took part in the Konitz–Koslin offensive, and in March in the Danzig offensive operation.

Mud was a constant hindrance to the movement of vehicles on the Eastern Front. Here a Sturmgeschütz III hauls a stranded Horch light cross-country vehicle through the mire.

and determination, they were constantly hampered by the lack of weapons and manpower needed to sustain them. Consequently, the remaining troops holding out in the town were subjected to merciless ground and aerial bombardments. When Konitz fell to the Soviets, some eight hundred German soldiers were dead, and the town was heavily damaged. Soviet spearheads then wheeled toward Koslin.

Over the last few days of February, German troops were slowly being pushed further back by overwhelming enemy firepower from both ground and aerial attacks. Despite Red Army superiority in the area, Hitler still insisted that his troops fight from fixed positions without the possibility of any tactical retreat. Therefore, the order caused many units to become encircled by Red Army rifle divisions, leaving T-34 tank units to speed past unhindered and

A column of Sturmgeschütz IIIs advances along a road bound for the front. The vehicles initially provided crucial mobile fire support to the infantry and proved their worth as an invaluable antitank weapon. By the end of 1944, the StuG was primarily used as an antitank weapon, thus depriving the infantry of vital fire support.

Two Soviet commanders in an American Jeep. Note the soldier armed with the PPS-43 submachine gun. Behind them is a T-34 tank loaded with infantry being carried to the forward edge of the battlefield.

Soviet troops enter a captured town in East Pomerania. Several of the towns were turned into fortresses and their strength varied considerably. Destroyed vehicles including a knocked-out Sturmgeschütz III litter the street. In urbanized fighting the StuG's effectiveness was curtailed as it did not have a conventional turret and its barrel was limited in traverse.

Being prepared for a fire mission is the 12cm Granatwerfer 42 (Grenade Thrower Model 42; official designation: 12cm GrW 42).

A Soviet 122mm howitzer 1938 M-30 being hauled by a caterpillar tractor STZ-5 Stalin along a typical road that has been turned into a quagmire from the thaw.

achieve deeper penetrations. Whilst many areas of the German front simply cracked under the sheer weight of the Soviet onslaught, several German units continued to demonstrate their ability to defend well. In front of Koslin German infantry divisions bitterly contested large areas of terrain. Fighting was often savage, resulting in terrible casualties on both sides. Yet, despite the heavy resistance, the Germans still lacked the strength to contain the enemy. The Red Army continued to exploit the terrain, driving back or encircling the Germans as

A column of T-34 85 tanks inside a forest for concealment. These tanks belong to the 7th Guards Tank Regiment, 49th Army.

they went. On the main road to Koslin, Soviet infantry fought doggedly against stiff German defenses. By March, Soviet units had finally broken through to Koslin, and the town fell on March 4. The reverberations caused by the loss of Koslin meant that the German Second Army found itself completely cut off from the rest of its army group. What followed was bitter fighting, as the entire left wing of the Third Panzer Army was virtually encircled.

As a result of the Red Army's offensive, the entire German front had been pierced in numerous places. Although considerable numbers of troops were trying to hold their positions, they were unable to avoid the inevitable encirclements that followed. Nevertheless, General Weiß was determined to try and hold his forces together by demanding that his units immediately stop withdrawing and maintain fresh lines of defense. However, the damage to his force was beyond repair.

What followed was forward Soviet tank units reaching the Baltic Sea, and the German forces in Pomerania being trapped in a series of encirclements. The Second Army was forced to withdraw toward Danzig, which had been hurriedly fortified, while the X SS Corps of

An SU-76 advances through a recently captured town, past burning buildings. The SU-76M was a multipurpose SPG and combined three main battlefield roles: light assault gun for infantry support, mobile antitank weapon, and mobile gun for indirect fire.

A crew pose for the camera in March 1945 with their Pz.Kpfw. IV Ausf.J. Foliage has been attached to the the vehicle to break up its distinctive shape. Even by the late-war period the Pz.Kpfw. IV was still the most common battle tank in the German arsenal.

the Third Panzer Army was surrounded at Dramburg. All the troops could do now to slow the Red Army on their drive to the Baltic was erect crude roadblocks and defense barriers. Signs of disintegration now plagued every part of the front, which was almost impossible to control. Although several sectors held their ground, large parts of the front were on the point of collapse. The 2nd Belorussian Front had now trapped massive numbers of the enemy, who were slowly and systematically being bled to death, in a pincer movement. For hours hapless German troops were subjected to merciless low-level strafing by Soviet fighter-bombers and blasted by artillery.

With Koslin captured and advanced spearheads reaching the coastal area of the Baltic, General Rokossovky could now open his second phase of the East Pomeranian offensive operation.

Panzer commanders converse over a map. In the background is a whitewashed Pz.Kpfw. IV with its *schürzen* side skirting missing or adrift.

Danzig Offensive, March 6–31, 1945

With the first phase completed, the 2nd Belorussian Front was tasked with the second phase, which opened on March 6, 1945. The objective was for the 2nd Shock Army to advance in a large pincer movement and capture the fortress of Marienburg. Robust Soviet attacks would also simultaneously spearhead its powerful formations to the east of Elbing and annihilate enemy troops there, with the final part of the plan seizing the city of Danzig, surrounding areas, and Gdingen.

Directive of the Stavka VGK No. 11035. To the Commander of the Second Belorussian Front on the Development of the Operation in East Prussia (via *Prelude to Berlin*):

> 5 March 1945, 2000
>
> The Stavka of the Supreme High Command orders:
>
> 1. The forces of the Second Belorussian Front are to defeat the enemy group of forces in the Danzig–Stolp area and capture the cities of Danzig and Gdynia, and no later than 20 March reach the coast of the Baltic Sea.

As the Red Army pushed west and to the Baltic coast, Volksdeutsche—ethnic Germans living outside Germany—begin fleeing their homes to escape the Soviets. Many of the refugees were evacuated from East Prussia (via Pillau or the Nehrung), first to Danzig or Gdynia/Gotenhafen and from there to the more westerly parts of Germany.

A column of Soviet armor bound for Danzig in early March 1945.

A column of T-34 tanks bound for Danzig. The Soviets were totally aware of the important strategic location of Danzig, the last German stronghold in the region.

An ad hoc Waffen-SS unit in front of Danzig, March 1945.

2. In order to carry out this task, the front's forces are to continue the offensive by the right wing along the western bank of the Vistula River toward Danzig, and along the left wing toward Lauenburg and Gdynia. The 1st Guards Tank Army and the Polish 1st Army's tank brigade are to be employed for developing the attack along the front's left wing.

3. As the coastline is cleared, organize its solid defense, employing for this purpose the 3rd Guards Cavalry Corps, fortified areas and other units.

4. The boundary lines and the responsibility for securing the boundaries with neighboring fronts are as before.

5. Report on orders issued.

Stavka of the Supreme High Command

I. Stalin

A. Antonov

Volkssturm militia during an oath ceremony in Danzig. Two men are armed with Panzerschreck antitank grenade launchers. The man on the left has an MG-42 machine gun.

The Danzig offensive operation was a general continuation of the East Pomeranian offensive, with Rokossovsky's troops not pausing between each phase, which also included simultaneously launching the Arnswalde–Kolberg offensive operation.

For the Danzig offensive, the 2nd Shock Army quickly gained momentum against disjointed enemy formations and drove at speed towards what was *Festung* Marienburg.

A teenage member of the Hitlerjugend distributes grenades to a motley group of *Volkssturm truppen* in Danzig. The weapons are a mix of Panzerfausts and old infantry rifles.

Civilians fleeing Danzig as the Soviets approach.

A Soviet 57mm ZiS-2 antitank gun being hauled by a truck moves through a town for the front.

Soviet artillery opens fire on Danzig with a M1931/37 (A-19) 122mm corps gun. By the late-war period, all new artillery regiments were issued 122mm guns along with other pieces, mainly 107mm guns and 152mm howitzers. In total there were sixteen to twenty pieces per regiment.

An ISU-152 halted in field prior to commencing operations through eastern Germany.

Fearing their defensive force would be cut off if they stood and defended the Teutonic castle, the *kampfgruppe* under the control of the staff of the depleted 7th Infantry Division, which included a motley collection of marine, Waffen-SS, and other units, immediately ordered the evacuation of the castle and took what weaponry they could to avoid complete annihilation. Units of the 2nd Belorussian Front continued the advance, combing the area and closing in on the edge of East Prussia at Elbing. Soviet soldiers increasingly encountered strong resistance, with towns and villages defended by a mixture of ad hoc battle groups comprising of Luftwaffe field troops, Waffen-SS, and Heer soldiers, and often bolstered by members of the civilian population pressganged into the *Volkssturm*. Many of the towns had been turned into fortified strongpoints. Fighting, where possible, was prolonged by the Germans. Though

Soviet self-propelled ISU-122 on Holtsraum Street in Danzig. These Soviet tank destroyers fired massive 25kg shells, with a muzzle velocity of 800 m/s, and were equipped with a 3kg TNT charge. Shock and explosions were often enough to knock out enemy AFVs with no armor protection. They were used extensively in urban fighting.

From the turret of an IS-2 Soviet tank belonging to the 62nd Guards Heavy Tank Regiment during street fighting in Danzig. Note the mounted 7.62mm DT machine gun.

A column of Soviet armored vehicles during the battle for Danzig drive through Karthauser-Straßein in the district of the Church of St. Francis Assizskogo. The stationary vehicle on the right is an ISU-122.

Soviet soldiers on board an IS-2 advance along a street during the battle for Danzig.

A T-34 rolls through a captured street in Danzig.

they had no realistic hope of victory and were severely short of manpower, ammunition, and fuel, they continued to offer credible resistance, inflicting high casualties on the Red Army.

High losses were also seen in areas where the Germans were encircled or trapped. In the Elbing Pocket, or what was better known as the Heiligenbeil *Kessel*, fighting had been raging since late January. The German Fourth Army, including some units of the Second Army, was encircled and was slowly and systematically being pounded into submission. Attempts by the Red Army to break through the German perimeter early in February were repulsed. However, despite dogged German resistance, General Weiß warned Hitler of the serious consequences of the situation and told his Führer that the pocket could not be held. On March 9 he was relieved of his command and replaced by General Dietrich von Saucken. This did not prevent troops of the Second Army withdrawing in total panic and confusion into Danzig and Gdingen, where they were besieged by the 2nd Belorussian Front. Zhukov's forces, meanwhile, cleared the remainder of Third Panzer Army from the east bank of the lower Oder, pushing back beleaguered German formations from the bridgehead at Altdamm.

A self-propelled ISU-122 inside Danzig. Note the devastation wrought on the city by the heavy Soviet artillery.

Local women and children evacuate Danzig as the fighting inside the city intensifies.

On March 15 the 2nd Belorussian Front drove along the Baltic, thrusting its units toward the coast at Zoppot between Gotenhafen and Danzig. To avert the capture of Zoppot and the nearby port of Gotenhafen, von Saucken quickly pulled together a force to defend the area, consisting of the VII Panzer Corps, XXXXV Army Corps, XXVII Army Corps, 251st Infantry Division, 4th SS Polizei Division, 7th Panzer Division, 215th Infantry Division, 32nd Infantry Division, 227th Infantry Division, 73rd Infantry Division, 389th Infantry Division, and the 252nd Infantry Division.

Whilst German forces in Zoppot and the immediate surrounding areas braced themselves for an enemy attack, the Soviet 70th and 49th Armies fought a series of engagements, forcing the 4th Panzer Division back to the outskirts of Danzig. The attack on the city proper began with a massive Soviet artillery bombardment that continued over the course of several days. The heavy shelling resulted in many of the buildings in the city center being destroyed, which resulted in several German defenses being knocked out

Soviet antiaircraft gunners from the 740th Artillery Regiment in an M-17 armored personnel carrier on the streets of liberated Danzig.

of action. As bombing intensified, a Fallschirmjäger unit was deployed in the nearby forest of Oliwa to draw off some of the pressure against Danzig. This provoked Soviet formations to enter the forest on March 18. What followed was a bloody battle which spanned seven days until the Red Army crushed all resistance, but at considerable cost in men.

The maintenance facility for s.SS.Pz.Abt. 503 (503rd SS Heavy Tank Battalion) was on the wharf at Danzig. When the Soviets entered the city, the unit reported knocking out six IS-2 tanks and capturing a seventh. The captured Red Army tank was then reused by the Germans for a short period before being disposed of in the harbor. During the battle for Danzig s.SS.Pz.Abt. 503 were reduced to just six operational Tiger IIs, with a further seven in for repair, leaving 13 Tiger IIs to fight. However, the main armored force in the city was the 35th Panzer Regiment, 4th Panzer Division. The first battalion was equipped with Panther tanks (3rd Company with Jagdpanthers), while the second battalion had PzKpfw IVs. The artillery regiment was equipped mainly with Wespe and Hummel self-propelled howitzers.

By 22 March, the 70th Army had reached the sea, separating Gotenhafen from the main German force east of Danzig. Three days later the 70th Army arrived at the Gulf of Danzig, with the 2nd Army vainly trying to stem the onslaught. However, despite the overwhelming Soviet might, German troops were still forbidden to concede further ground along the Baltic. As a consequence, on March 26, Gotenhafen fell, but at terrible cost to both sides. Many civilians were killed during the battle, and those who had managed to survive retreated to the headland at Oksywie along with remnants of the defenders, to be evacuated to the Hel Peninsula.

As the surrounding areas were cleared of German defenses, the 2nd Guards Tank Army directed its assault on Danzig. To Hitler, Danzig was of great historical importance. The city was defended by German units comprising elements of the 4th Panzer Division and various other Heer and Kriegsmarine personnel supported by *Volkssturm* and Hitlerjugend *truppen*. They were determined to defend the city, as their Führer had ordered every man to do his duty and fight to the death. The 4th Panzer Division carried the bulk of the defense, which consisted of panzer and artillery regiments equipped with Panthers and Pz.Kpfw. IVs plus Wespe and Hummel self-propelled howitzers.

A German Pak gun in action, Danzig.

A knocked-out Tiger II tank from 503rd SS Heavy Tank Battalion *or SS.Pz.Abt. 503* has evidently fallen into a sinkhole. Note the Soviet IS-2 tank in the background.

The first sighting of Soviet infantry entering the suburbs was on March 24. Two days later the city was engulfed in bitter and bloody fighting. The situation inside the city became increasingly disorganized. Communication networks no longer existed, and orders were now issued by word of mouth. The chaos was so bad that officers arriving to take over units soon discovered they had nothing to take over, because their commands had already been captured or annihilated. In most areas, well-armed soldiers were left leaderless and did not know exactly where they were fighting. Street by street, house by house, fighting intensified, with many German soldiers being captured or wounded. Other demoralized groups of soldiers who had run out of ammunition simply broke and ran, trying to escape westward. The few remaining soldiers who stood resolute were steadily driven back into the center

The destruction of Danzig following its capture at the end of March 1945 was almost absolute.

Ruined buildings on the Westerplatte in Danzig.

of the city. In the vast city wasteland, the once-broad streets were now pitted paths that crisscrossed mountains of rubble. This was where the last German troops held out, regularly exposed to heavy fire, with no support, and in many cases they were quickly encircled and destroyed.

The German defense of Danzig began to crumble on March 28, after which the remnants of th Second Army withdrew to the delta of the Vistula River to the northeast of the city. Evacuation of civilians and military personnel from there and from the Hel Peninsula continued until the end of the Soviet offensive.

According to the Red Army, the battle of Danzig claimed the loss of thirty-nine thousand German soldiers and ten thousand captured. Danzig had been an important strategic location and the last German stronghold in the region. Its capture was a blow to

A column of IS-122 tank destroyers entering the city following its capture. Polish troops are in the Jeep in the foreground.

Soviet armor during a break.

Hitler's strategic plan, and with the fall of Zoppot and Gotenhafen as well, he reluctantly conceded during a military briefing that the situation along the Baltic was so perilous that an invasion of the Reich was imminent.

March 1945 was crucial to the Soviet military success in the north and critical for the main Soviet drive to the Oder River. Whilst parts of the 2nd Belorussian Front had been successfully engaging the Germans along the Baltic Sea toward the Hel Peninsula, Gotenhafen, Danzig, Pillau, the Frische Nehrung and trying to reduce the German corridor between East Prussia and Königsberg, Rokossovsky was also directing his forces simultaneously to take Arnswalde and Kolberg.

A German Nebelwerfer rocket launcher being towed by a halftrack. These weapons were often organized into batteries of six launchers, with three batteries per battalion. These battalions were concentrated in independent *Werfer-Regimenter* and *Brigaden*.

Arnswalde–Kolberg Offensive, March 1–18, 1945

As the Konitz–Koslin offensive operation progressed, formations from Zhukov's 1st Belorussian Front and Rokossovsky's 2nd Belorussian Front launched an operation aimed at taking the Arnswalde and Kolberg areas. One of the main cities in Pomerania was Kolberg; it was one of the key German positions in the Pomeranian Wall and a vital link between Pomerania and Prussia. The German high command had planned to use the port facilities there for the logistical supply of nearby German forces, and hoped that the presence of this stronghold would lure Soviet forces away from the main thrust toward Berlin. What followed was the Arnswalde–Koblerg operation that led to the brutal battle of Kolberg.

Winter-clad grenadiers wearing their two-piece smocks. One is dragging a sled.

German troops in a defensive position in a town. The soldier by the tree is armed with a Panzerfaust.

Directive of the Stavka VGK No. 11034. To the Commanders of the First and Second Belorussian Fronts on the Temporary Resubordination of the 1st Guards Tank Army:

> 5 March 1945, 2000 hrs
>
> The Stavka of the Supreme High Command orders:
>
> Following the elimination of the enemy in the Belgard–Kolberg area, but no later than 8 March, the First Belorussian Front's 1st Guards Tank Army will be

An 8.8cm Flak gun being manually loaded onto its two-wheeled limbers known as the Sonderanhangar 202. The limbers could be removed after lowering the platform by hand winches.

Soviet troops queue for food at an outdoor kitchen facility.

temporarily subordinated to the Second Belorussian Front, with the inclusion of the Polish 1st Army's tank brigade.

2. The army is to be transferred intact, with all its reinforcement equipment, army rear units and establishments, with two refills of fuel and three refills of diesel fuel.

3. The commander of the Second Belorussian Front should keep in mind that the 1st Guards Tank Army, minus the Polish tank brigade, must be returned to the First Belorussian Front by no later than 24 March.

4. Report on fulfilment.

Stavka of the Supreme High Command

I. Stalin

A. Antonov

A German quadruple flak gun being readied for action in the snow.

A German Panzerwerfer battery opens fire on Soviet positions. The Panzerwerfer 42 auf Maultier was used for larger-scale rocket barrages in areas not requiring accurate artillery fire.

A Soviet machine gunner in his winter whites mans his Pulyemyot Maksima PM1910.

A column of Soviet IS-2 tanks rolls through a captured town. Note the makeshift German defenses erected in the road.

An IS-2 tank crew pose on their stationary vehicle in a captured town.

Wounded Soviet soldiers hitching a ride on a T-34 tank.

Soviet troops on the march along a muddy road. Heavy traffic has turned the already boggy dirt track into a quagmire as the snow thaws.

For the offensive, the Red Army and supporting Polish forces were divided into two waves. The first was comprised of units of the Red Army, and the second formations of General Major Stanislav G. Poplavsky's Polish 1st Army of the 1st Belorussian Front. The principal Soviet units were the 45th Tank Brigade and the 272nd Division. The Polish units, totaling more than twenty-eight thousand men, included the Polish 6th Division, 3rd Division, 4th Division, and several support units.

A Soviet SU-76 crosses a river. The SU-76M virtually replaced light tanks in the close-support role by mid-war. Each light self-propelled gun regiment was equipped with 21 SU-76Ms; there were 119 such regiments in the Red Army by March 1945.

An SU-76 being loaded with ammunition. Ammunition types included armor-piercing hollow charge, high explosive, fragmentation, shrapnel, and incendiary projectiles, which made the SU-76 an excellent multipurpose light armored fighting vehicle.

More than likely a staged photograph showing Soviet soldiers charging into action supported by a battery of SU-76s, March 1945. The SU-76 was well regarded by Soviet troops. It had a more powerful gun than any previous light tank for close support of infantry in defensive and offensive operations.

An ISU-122 heavy self-propelled gun rolls by a dead German soldier in the road.

South of Kolberg lay the town of Arnswalde, which was in the path of Zhukov's forces. Some of Zhukov's units had been diverted north in early February 1945 to assist in clearing Pomerania up to the Baltic Sea. As Zhukov's spearheads drove north, they advanced toward the town of Arnswalde. The town itself was strategically important to the Germans as it was a vital hub for Kolberg and the north. Defense of Arnswalde initially came under the command of General Hans Voigt's *Kampfgruppe*, and was made up of three thousand Nebelwerfer replacement troops, and two thousand three hundred fresh troops just out of training. The newly arrived Waffen-SS tanks from elements of the 503rd SS Heavy Tank Battalion *or SS.Pz.Abt. 503*—four Tiger II tanks—were ordered to keep the city's route to the north open. For days, fighting raged in and around the town, with Voigt's *Kampfgruppe* fighting doggedly to hold off the relentless Soviet attacks. As the fighting intensified, the *Kampfgruppe* was reinforced by another two Tiger II tanks and 10 StuG assault guns from the 11th SS Panzer Division Nordland, as well as a company of

An IS-122 heavy self-propelled gun crosses a stream. Red Army commanders viewed the ISU-122 as a robust assault gun that was especially effective in destroying German defensive positions.

Soldiers of the Polish 1st Army Tank Brigade advance on Kolberg supported by a column of T-34 tanks. Stavka, on March 5, outlined that following the elimination of the enemy in the Belgard–Kolberg area, but no later than March 8, the 1st Belorussian Front's 1st Guards Tank Army would be temporarily subordinated to the 2nd Belorussian Front, with the inclusion of the Polish 1st Army Tank Brigade.

A Waffen-SS tank crew on board a stationary Sd.Kfz. 10/4 during operations near Kolberg.

A column of Soviet tanks enters Kolberg. The Germans succeeded in evacuating much of their military personnel and refugees from the city via sea before it was taken by the Poles on March 18, 1945.

Polish troops engage German defensive units during the battle of Kolberg.

Fallschirmjäger. By this time the town was completely encircled, and the Germans knew that if they stayed, they would be defending it to their deaths. As a result, several German attacks were made toward the town in order to relieve it and allow troops and civilians to withdraw. The last troops were withdrawn from Arnswalde on February 22. The town fell later that day.

Soviet plans were immediately drawn up for an all-out offensive north against Kolberg, using the town as a springboard against enemy troop concentrations in the area. The offensive operation against Kolberg was launched on March 1, with Zhukov's forces advancing north and clashing with retreating German formations which were trying desperately to establish

A wounded Polish soldier is carried to a field dressing station during the battle for Kolberg.

Polish troops hurry forward amid the ruins during the battle for Kolberg. The Polish 1st Army had been tasked with taking the city. However, German resistance was strong and the initial attacks into the city were repulsed.

a cohesive defensive line. As the Red Army bore down on Kolberg, the city was further strengthened; it was known as *Festung* Kolberg. Although Hitler regarded the city as a vital link between Pomerania and East Prussia and an important resupply port, in his eyes Kolberg was more than just a city of strategic importance: only weeks before, in February, the Propaganda Minister Joseph Goebbels had released a movie called *Kolberg*, which was a color epic depicting Gneisenau's successful defense of the city against the French in 1807. The movie was lavishly filmed; some one hundred thousand Wehrmacht troops had been taken from the front to star in the famous battle's reproduction. It was shown in cinemas all over Germany in a drastic attempt to enthuse determination and fighting spirit across the nation.

Defending the city were various ad hoc formations from Army Group Vistula, which had arrived in the city in late February after continuously fighting off heavy Soviet attacks from East Prussia and from Arnswalde in the south. Most German soldiers were already exhausted, and were low on ammunition and equipment. Newly arrived forces which had come to defend the city comprised the Third Panzer Army (with 18 tanks), 33rd Waffen-SS

The destruction of Kolberg.

A German 8.8cm Flak gun being used in a ground role, set up on a bridge during the battles for Altdamm.

Grenadier Division Charlemagne (1st French), and the 15th Waffen-SS Grenadier Division (1st Latvian), supported by a mixture of some ten thousand *Volkssturm* and Hitlerjugend conscripts and various local militia and volunteers. Surprisingly the Germans also received supplies by air and sea, and were supported by naval gunfire from the pocket battleships *Lützow* and *Admiral Scheer*, and bizarrely, an armored gun train.

The Red Army offensive began in earnest at dawn on March 4, with a barrage of heavy bombardments and simultaneous infantry assaults by units of the 1st and 2nd Belorussian Fronts. However, the initial assaults were weak, and the Germans were able to repulse them. It was not until the nearby town of Koslin was captured by the Soviets that additional reinforcements could be used against *Festung* Kolberg.

A destroyed Tiger II with its dead crew scattered around it. Four Tiger II tanks were expected to keep Kolberg's connection to the north open.

Two photographs taken in sequence showing a T-34 tank moving along a street following the capture of Kolberg.

Over the next few days, Soviet and Polish forces launched a series of attacks against the city. The Poles had been given the task of capturing Kolberg, and it was the 3rd Polish Infantry Division, along with supporting units, that attempted to storm the city. Fighting inside the city became a battle of attrition: *Volkssturm* and Hitlerjugend soldiers had become masters of defense. Losses on both sides were high. Fighting was merciless, and the battle continued to rage night and day, with stubborn German fighters defending every yard of ground.

On 12 March a fresh assault was launched by the

A Soviet column halted on a street in Kolberg at the end of March 1945. Note the M1940 (72-K) 25mm automatic air defense gun. The 72-K was designed for antiaircraft defense for infantry regiments.

Poles, this time with additional armor and artillery, including the 4th Polish Infantry Division. For two days the Poles and German defenders were heavily embroiled in bitter combat. However, despite serious losses and the fact that they were slowly running out of ammunition, the Germans refused to surrender. The defense of the city was so vital that additional reinforcements from the Kell battalions at Swinemünde were rushed to the city to prevent a collapse. But the Red Army pressure was relentless, and by March 16 the Germans had reluctantly pulled back most of their forces to concentrate on the defense of the port. The following day most of the German lines were abandoned, leaving small groups of troops to hold the line whilst the bulk of the defenders began evacuating to Swinemünde. The evacuation was undertaken by the Kriegsmarine in what was known as Operation *Hannibal*. Some forty thousand German soldiers and seventy thousand refugees were successfully evacuated from Kolberg.

With the evacuation of the last remaining forces in Kolberg, the city finally fell on 18 March. When the Poles marched into the city, they found it almost unrecognizable, with the city utterly destroyed by the heavy ground and aerial bombardments.

Although Hitler looked upon the battle of Kolberg as a complete disaster, the majority of the troops defending the city had managed to escape destruction. However, the aftermath of the battle saw the German defense of East Pomerania begin its inexorable collapse. Exhausted and demoralized German troops began withdrawing west, intermingled with tens of thousands of civilians on foot trying to reach the congested ports along the Baltic like Pillau and Nehrung in East Prussia. From here the boats would first transport the evacuees to Danzig or Gotenhafen, and from there to Germany proper. The overcrowding was so bad that great numbers risked their lives by crossing the frozen eastern Baltic from East Prussia and Danzig. The Soviet Air Force would then sweep over the columns of fleeing civilians. Women and children cowered as the pilots dropped their bombs, breaking the ice and plunging hundreds into the freezing water.

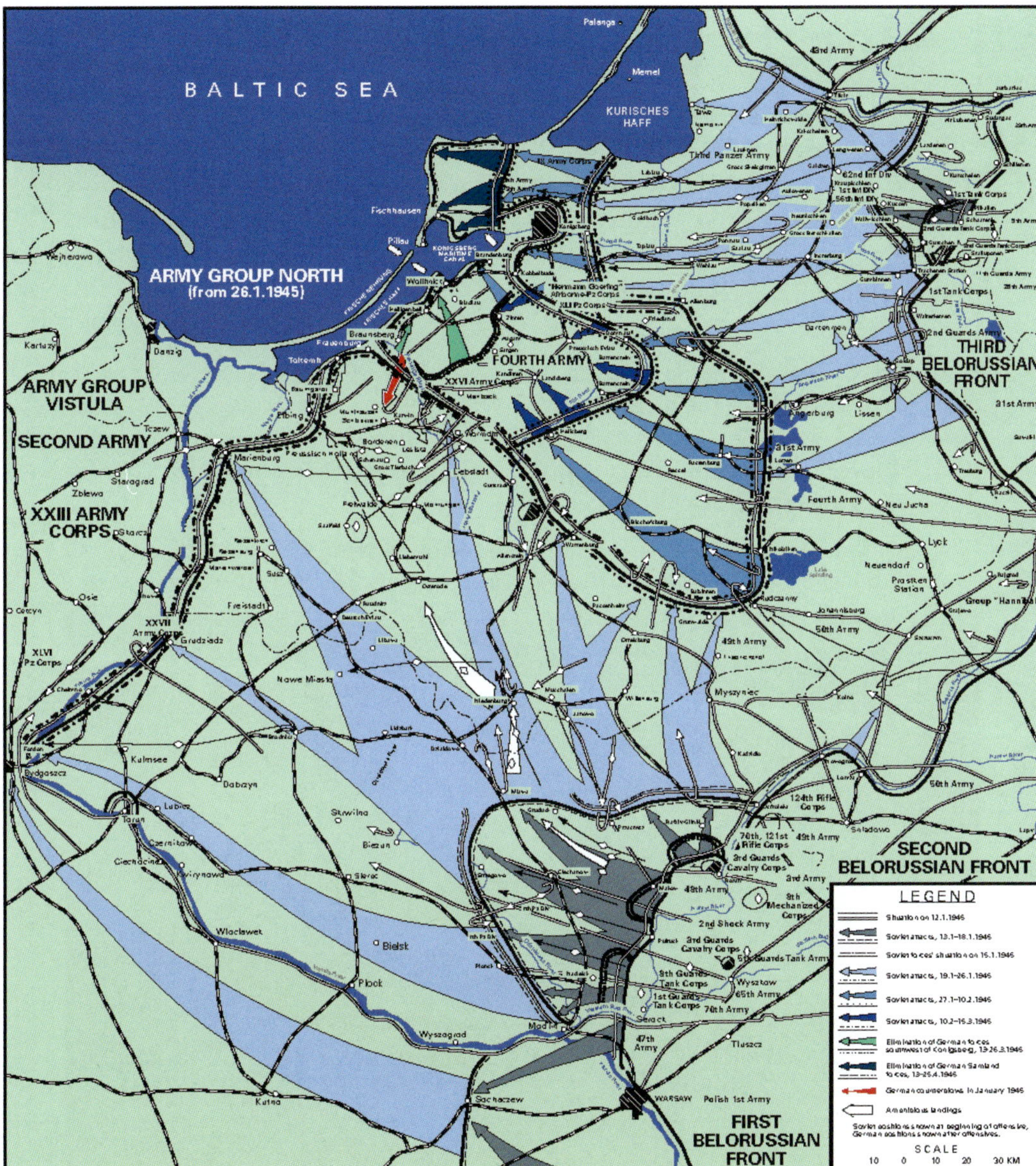

Combat activities in the East Prussia operation (January 13–April 25, 1945).

Altdamm Offensive, March 18–April 4, 1945

During the Arnswalde–Kolberg offensive several Soviet formations of Rokossovsky's 2nd Belorussian Front began to deploy west to replace the troops of Zhukov's 1st Belorussian Front along what was known as the "Kolberg line," the Oder River estuary, and farther along the eastern bank of the river as far as Schwedt.

It was in this region that the Soviet leadership proposed to group three of its Soviet armies in the Altdamm area of the Schwedt sector. What followed was the last phase in East Pomerania, known as the Altdamm offensive operation. The operation consisted of a plan to send advancing spearheads of the 1st Belorussian Front against the German 11th SS Panzer Army, which was being assembled in Pomerania.

Supporting the ground forces of the 2nd Belorussian Front were the 4th Assault Air Army's 8th Fighter and 5th Bomber Corps. Between them they had some one thousand

Three Soviet infantrymen, two certainly middle-aged, pose for the camera armed with PPSh-41 submachine guns.

An SU-152 commander speaking to his crew. By early 1945, the SU-152 was incorporated into guards heavy self-propelled artillery brigades to provide fire support to the tank armies. These were organized along the tank brigade model, each with 65 ISU-152 or ISU-122 self-propelled guns.

three hundred aircraft, of which five hundred were fighters, with another five hundred being assault aircraft, two hundred and sixty of which were bombers (one hundred and ten of these bombers were Po-2 aircraft), and forty of which were reconnaissance planes. This massive assemblage of aircraft was required to soften a stubborn a German defense which consisted of a powerful infantry group, with two hundred panzers and assault guns, one hundred and eighty artillery batteries and mortars, and a hundred or so aircraft.

An SU-76 travels along a cobbled road.

An SU-76 inside a captured village preparing to redeploy. The SU-76 was effective against any medium or light German tank. It could also knock out the Panther tank with a flank shot, but was ineffective against Tiger tanks.

The last phase of the offensive was launched on March 18 with units of the 4th Air Army's 8th Fighter Corps carrying out a series of attacks against German defenses and airfields. As a result, 64 Luftwaffe planes were destroyed or put out of action. Following the aerial attack, the front's ground mobile formations launched a series of successive attacks. Red Army units soon became embroiled in heavy fighting, with some formations penetrating some of the German defensive positions. The VII Panzer Corps took a heavy battering, as the Soviets successfully breached several defenses. German front lines were either in turmoil or being ruptured by Soviet assault units. The smoldering town of Stettin-Altdamm was being held by III SS Panzer Corps, which had retreated to the area and was being defended by remnants of the 10th, 11th, 23rd, 27th, and 28th SS Divisions and a panzer *kampfgruppe* with two Panthers, four Pz.Kpfw. IVs, and two Sturmgeschütz. The battle group was supported by a *schwere* (heavy) panzer platoon with one Königstiger and an *SS-Gepanzerte* panzergrenadier platoon with artillery, and a Luftwaffe heavy flak platoon.

A German soldier tucks into his mess tin during a pause in the fighting.

A battery of ISU-122 tank destroyers advancing across open terrain. The ISU-122 had good armor performance and was particularly lethal with its high-explosive rounds.

Slowly and systematically the Soviets bulldozed their way through the lines at Stettin, crushing ad hoc Waffen-SS lines and reaching Altdamm. What followed were Red Army IS-2 and T34 tanks that clashed with the panzer platoon in the town. Although the initial Soviet attack failed with the loss of some 18 vehicles, the Germans were aware that they could not hold their positions for any appreciable length of time. As a result, the remnants of the panzer *kampgruppe* and panzergrenadier platoons withdrew, leaving the Soviets to capture the town on March 20.

The Soviet 2nd Shock Army, together with the 8th Guards Tank Corps, began penetrating areas westward along the Baltic, launching attacks in the general direction of Danzig, from the south. The 65th Army, supported by the 8th Mechanized Corps, then broke through the main defensive line along the Radaune River near Danzig. The 49th Army, along with the 1st Guards Tank Corps, fought a series of battles against stiff German

A trio of Soviet ISU-122s below a crest in ambush position.

A Sturmgeschütz commander poses with his assault gun during a pause in operations. The vehicle still retains its summer camouflage scheme, as many units did not have adequate supplies of winter whitewash.

opposition along the Barnewitz–Neue Welt sector and broke through. Fighting in the area intensified as the Soviets exploited the receding front by methodically reducing the German defenses to rubble. The Soviet attacks were intense and without respite. Hitler's insistence that his troops fight from fixed positions without the option of tactical retreat caused many units to become encircled by Red Army rifle divisions, leaving tank units to speed past unhindered and achieve deeper penetrations. The success of these breakthroughs saw the

Civilians fleeing west to escape the Red Army.

A column of IS-2 tanks advances along a road. Note the abandoned German Volkswagen Type 82, which has either developed a fault or more than likely run out of fuel.

An IS-122 self-propelled gun in a field after breaking cover from a row of trees. Note the gunner at the ready with the mounted 12.7mm DShK AA machine gun.

A T-34 tank has reached a river. Note the foliage attached to the vehicle to help break up its distinctive shape.

Standing in the cupola of his s.SS.Pz.Abt. 503 Tiger tank, the commander makes a radio antennae hand signal.

This Tiger II tank crew belonging to SS-Panzer-Abteilung 503 pose for the camera. The limited number of these heavy tanks, coupled with their specialized role in either offensive or defensive operations, meant they were not often permanently assigned to a single division or corps, but rather constantly moved from one flashpoint to the next.

Soviet 70th Army, while operating with the 3rd Guards Tank Corps, break through towards the Gdynia (Gotenhafen/Gdingen) defensive area, capture the town of Zoppot, and reach the Bay of Danzig. As a result, the German forces were forced to split into two: Danzig and Gdingen.

Over the course of three days the 2nd Belorussian Front pulverized the separated Danzig and Gdingen groups. The 2nd Shock, 65th, 49th, and 70th Armies attacked the Germans' Danzig group, while the 19th Army and a corps from the 70th Army from the 1st Guards Tank Army engaged the Gdingen group. On March 26 the German Danzig group began withdrawing its armor and artillery into the fortress city. The 49th Army followed in

A staged photograph showing two Soviet soldiers in a foxhole. One is armed with the PPSh 41 submachine gun, whilst his comrade is clutching what appears to be a Soviet RGD-33 hand grenade.

A grenadier uses a stationary Pz.Kpfw. IV for cover during a heavy bombardment.

A Soviet IS-2 heavy tank advancing along a dirt road. Foliage is attached to the rear of the vehicle to break up its distinctive shape.

A pair of T-34-85 tanks advance along a road.

A Soviet armored column together with artillery is being directed through a captured town which is still burning following a heavy bombardment.

A Soviet Sherman M4 tank crew pose for a photo. By 1945, some Red Army armored units were standardized to depend primarily on the Sherman and not on T-34s.

This elderly *Volkssturm* soldier is armed with a bolt-action rifle.

A Sturmgeschütz on the battlefield. The StuG assault guns were cost-effective compared with the heavier German tanks and engaged enemy tanks with much success. However, they were called upon more and more and by 1945 many of them were lost in combat. Note the heavy *schürzen*, still in mint condition.

A Sturmgeschütz III with intact *schürzen* traveling through a rural area.

Soviet infantry march through a destroyed town on their westward advance. One soldier swings his guitar.

T-34-85 tanks of the 7th Guards Tank Corps taking advantage of a forest for concealment.

Soviet troops have hitched a lift aboard a T-34-85. At the battlefield these soldiers would dismount and go into action.

A Soviet artillery crew preparing their 122mm M3 howitzer against German positions inside a town.

pursuit and, although held back by stubborn enemy resistance, it soon reached the outskirts of Danzig and became engaged in street fighting.

As the battle for Danzig raged, the Soviets also concentrated their efforts against the German Gdingen group. The Soviet 19th Army fought a series of intense battles but by

A Soviet battery of 122mm M30 howitzers during a fire mission against German positions.

March 28 had captured Gdingen and the suburbs of Grabau, Kielau, and Zissau. In spite of the loss of Gdingen and other towns and villages in the surrounding area, the Gdingen group tried to maintain their positions, but were ruthlessly reduced. To stave off total annihilation, remnants of the German Second Army, demoralized and with virtually no weapons, withdrew along the Ochsheft beachhead, with no prospect of escape. The Soviet 19th Army then launched a series of attacks against the trapped enemy, and bit by bit the troops either surrendered or were killed. By April 4 what was left of the Second Army had been completely routed, which ended the fourth stage of the East Pomeranian offensive. Although remnants still resisted on the Putziger Nehrung spit and in the Vistula River delta southeast of Danzig, the soldiers were trapped and were no longer regarded as a threat to overall operations in Pomerania. The Germans there would not surrender until May 9.

Operations in East Pomerania had now been completed. Stalin himself announced to the commanders of the 1st and 2nd Belorussian Fronts that the German forces in East Pomerania had been successfully routed. He ordered the 2nd Shock Army to complete clearing operations in area. The defeat of the German Second Army and the total capture of East Pomerania were secured. The arrival of the Red Army at the Baltic from the Bay of Danzig to the Bay of Stettin had now securely covered the flank of the Red Army preparing for the final drive on Berlin.

Soviet troops from the 311st Infantry Division in Altdamm following its capture.

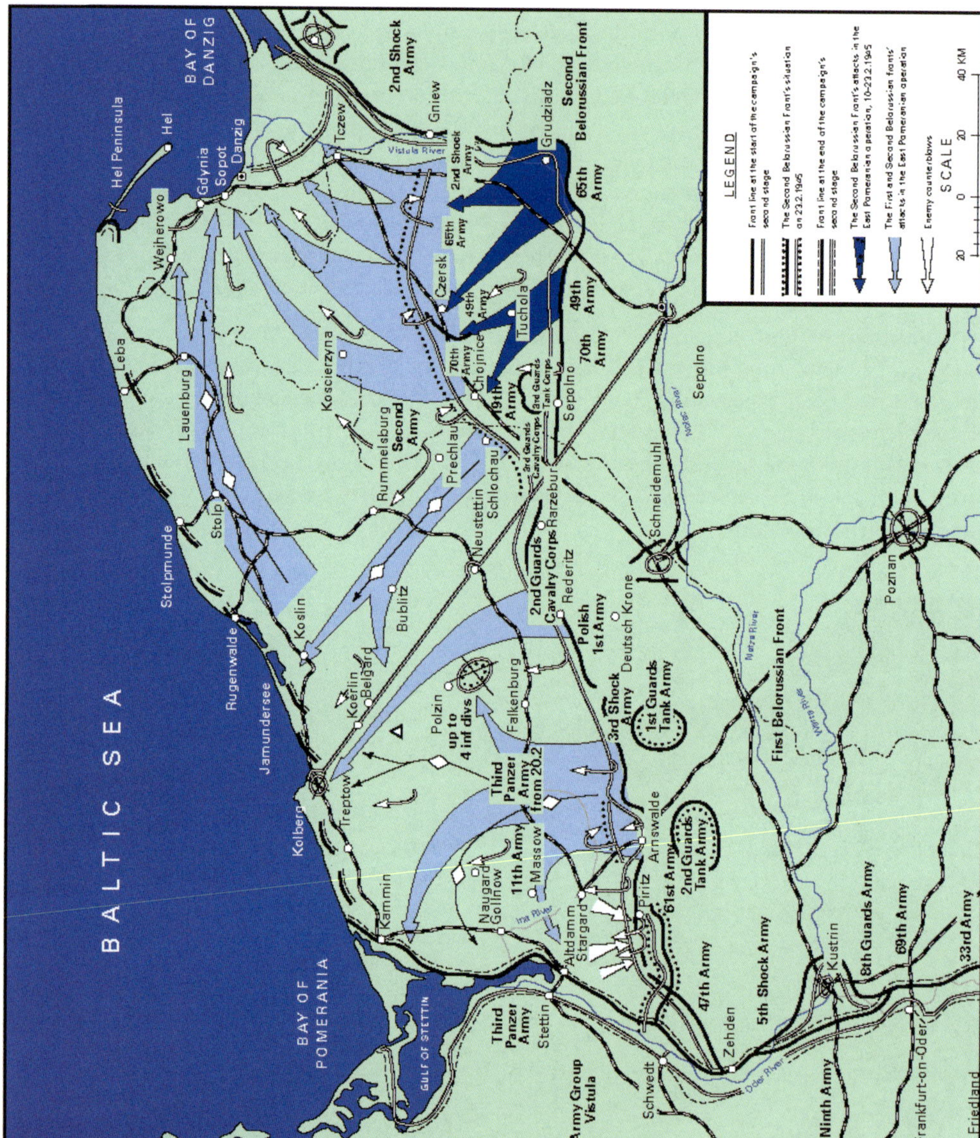

The Soviet offensive in Eastern Pomerania, Silesia and the Carpathians, February–March 1945.

Aftermath

By the end of March 1945, the German military situation in East Pomerania had deteriorated further, in spite of fanatical resistance. The position had become so bad that Hitler reluctantly allowed the Fourth Army to retreat across the Frisches Haff to the Nehrung. The army reported that it only had sixty thousand able-bodied men, and seventy thousand wounded. Hitler ordered that only the seriously wounded were to be evacuated; the remainder were to be used as replacements as they recovered.

In early April Hitler scraped together remnants of the Second and Fourth Armies and named the newly combined force the Army East Prussia. Members of this force were now fighting for their lives in and around the Bay of Danzig from Samland and Königsberg to the mouth of the Vistula. The remnants of two corps were given the task of holding positions north of Gotenhafen/Gdingen on the Hel Peninsula. Hitler demanded that these positions be held, and held at all costs. He instructed all forces in the Army East Prussia and Army Kurland to stay in position to draw the maximum number of enemy forces possible away from the main Soviet drive on Berlin.

In the first two weeks of April, as Army East Prussia tried to maintain its unstable position in the north, the Red Army consolidated its forces into three powerful fronts with the main front directed against Berlin. In the north, the 2nd Belorussian Front was to cross the Oder north of Schwedt and strike toward Neustrelitz. Its thrust was intended to drive the defending Third Panzer Army back against the coast and cover the advance toward Berlin on the northern flank. German forces, however, were determined to try and hold their positions

T-34-85 tanks of the 1st Belorussian Front stopped inside a captured town. With much of East Pomerania captured by the Soviets, Zhukov's 1st Belorussian Front was given the task of moving up to the Oder and preparing for the battle of Berlin.

Knocked-out German armor on the side of a road, evidence of the huge losses the Germans incurred as units tried to escape the overwhelming Soviet superiority in Pomerania.

for as long as possible and prevent the Soviets from taking possession of German territory. But the Germans no longer had the men or ammunition to defend their positions effectively. The Third Panzer Army had 11 remaining divisions, whilst the 2nd Belorussian Front had 8 armies totaling 33 rifle divisions, 4 tank and mechanized corps, and 3 artillery divisions plus a mixture of artillery and rocket-launcher brigades and regiments.

By mid-April the 2nd Belorussian Front had dislodged the Third Panzer Army from its defensive positions above the city of Stettin. Inside Stettin the city had been turned into one of Hitler's *festungen* and was being defended by "Fortress Division Stettin," which was comprised of an ad hoc mixture of *truppen* scraped together from the 3rd Panzer Army and supported by Hitlerjugend, *Volkssturm*, and Luftwaffe field soldiers. Though the Fortress Division had minimal armor and weaponry, it was able to fight well and repel several Soviet assaults until it finally capitulated on April 26. Many soldiers from the *Festung* were able to escape total encirclement and withdrew west to later surrender to British forces.

The withdrawal of the last remnants of the Army East Prussia to the west ended the primary operations for the 2nd Belorussian Front in East Pomerania. Although several towns and cities still held out through dogged German resistance, the war on the Eastern Front was essentially concluded.

The East Prussian operation had been a complicated offensive. It was an operation that had rolled over from the Red Army's winter offensive operations, which had begun in mid-January 1945, and as a result of which the 2nd and 3rd Belorussian Fronts had defeated the Germans over the course of some six weeks. The Soviet success in East Pomerania led to the 1st Belorussian Front and 1st Ukrainian Front reaching the Oder River on the approaches to Berlin and other areas of central Germany. The offensive in East Pomerania saw the Soviets drive west and north to the Baltic Sea, crushing enemy resistance and capturing key *Festungen* such as Kolberg and Danzig. As a result of the capture of East Pomerania and the arrival of Soviet formations along the Baltic, the 2nd Belorussian Front occupied virtually all East Pomerania, an area of some fourteen thousand squares miles. During the operation, some sixty towns and three hundred and fifty-five railroad stations, of which thirty-four were junctions, were captured.

The German Second Army, which was absorbed into the newly created Army East Prussia in early April, was destroyed, its remnants limping west into Western Allied territory and surrendering. The Red Army captured vast amounts of military equipment including some 680 tanks and self-propelled guns, 3,450 guns and mortars, 24,000 motor vehicles, and 430 aircraft. Along the Baltic coast, the Soviets captured 610 marine workshops, barracks, and other related buildings. Some 50 noncombat-ready U-boats were also captured plus 277 other vessels. The Red Army destroyed 2 panzer divisions, 1 panzer group, 15 infantry divisions, 10 infantry brigades, 84 independent battalions, 22 independent infantry regiments, and 2 military schools.

The annihilation of these German forces was due to the fluidity and rapid advance of the Red Army into East Pomerania. Soviet planners had ensured that the offensive would be uninterrupted. By not pausing between the January winter offensive and the East Pomeranian operations, the enemy would not be able to establish adequate lines of defense and would be wholly on the defensive without reprieve from attack. By the time the main Red Army spearheads arrived at Danzig and Gdingen, some Soviet armies were attacking along sectors up to seven miles in width and using heavy artillery bombardments and large-scale infantry charges to achieve their objectives. Red Army commanders owed much of their success to the employment of tank formations at various stages of the operation. Attached to these tank formations were motorized infantry and infantry supply units. This was a unique Red Army tactic in the latter part of the war which allowed tank formations to break free of the main attacking army and race ahead to achieve maximum ground. In fact, at one stage of the operation the 3rd Guards Tank Corps, for instance, had outstripped the 19th Army by more

A female Soviet soldier poses in front of a destroyed Hummel. The damage to the vehicle is extensive.

A knocked-out halftrack mounting a quadruple gun near a river in East Pomerania. A dead crewmember lies near the vehicle.

than fifty miles. Such advances often necessitated that the tanks halted and regrouped so the infantry and rear echelons could catch up.

Another major reason for the Soviet success of the offensive in East Pomerania was the role of artillery. As with many of the Soviet offensives, especially from 1943 onward, Soviet artillery was skillfully employed to achieve major breakthroughs. Often artillery and aerial support were undertaken simultaneously during the opening of an attack. However, the weather conditions during the East Pomeranian offensive were poor and Red Army Air Force operations were limited. But despite the unfavorable weather conditions, the 4th Air Army was able to successfully support ground operations, especially in and around Danzig and on the Hel Peninsula.

The Second Belorussian Front's East Pomeranian offensive had been successfully concluded with its armies' rapid offensive along the Baltic coast, which enabled the 1st Belorussian Front to defeat the powerful Eleventh Army, and the 2nd Belorussian Front to destroy the Second Army. Following the defeat of both German amies, the Stavka reoriented the 2nd Belorussian Front onto the Stettin axis on April 15, to prepare for operations against Berlin. Its orders were to launch an attack towards Stettin and Rostock, defeat the German Third Panzer Army, and secure the right flank of the 1st Belorussian Front, which had been given the task of attacking Berlin from the Oder River.

Between April 13 and 17, elements of the 2nd Belorussian Front replaced parts of the 1st Belorussian Front and prepared for their offensive. From north to south, the 2nd Belorussian Front deployed General Romanovsky's 19th Army on the coast to move west onto the peninsula directly to the east of the island of Usedom, whilst General Fedyuninsky's 2nd Shock Army was to capture Stettin and advance via Friedland to Stransund on the coast to the west of Usedom. General Popov's 70th Army and General Grishin's 49th Army were to operate as a shock group and take the area immediately to the south of Stettin before advancing to the west and northwest to seize Ribnitz, Wismar, and Ludwigslust and Lenzen on the Elbe River, respectively.

German Order of Battle, April 12, 1945

Third Panzer Army

III SS Panzer Corps (formally part of Army Group Vistula)

11th SS Panzergrenadier Division Nordland

23rd SS Panzergrenadier Division Nederland

28th SS Division Wallonien

27th SS Division Langemarck

XXXXVI Panzer Corps

1st Marine Infantry Division

547th Volksgrenadier Division

Gruppe Klosseck

XXXII Army Corps

281st Infantry Division

Fortress Stettin

549th Volksgrenadier Division

Gruppe Voigt

3rd Marine Infantry Division

Army of East Prussia (formerly Second Army)

Army East Prussia (*Armeeoberkommando Ostpreußen*, abbreviated *AOK Ostpreußen*) was created from the AOK 2nd Army and absorbed the remnants of the 4th Army on April 7, 1945. *AOK Ostpreußen* controlled all the troops in East and West Prussia.

Reserves

102nd Infantry Division

10th Jäger Brigade

349th Volksgrenadier Division

61st Infantry Division

69th Infantry Division

367th Infantry Division

548th Volksgrenadier Division

Hela Defenses

31st Volksgrenadier Division

4th SS Panzergrenadier Division Polizei

7th Infantry Division

203rd Infantry Division

83rd Infantry Division

XXIII Army Corps

4th Panzer Division

252nd Infantry Division

12th Luftwaffe Field Division

35th Infantry Division

23rd Infantry Division

32nd Infantry Division

XVIII Mountain Corps

7th Infantry Division

XXVI Army Corps

5th Panzer Division (includes remnants of 561st Volksgrenadier Division)

21st Infantry Division

1st Infantry Division

58th Infantry Division

28th Jäger Division

IX Army Corps

93rd Infantry Division

95th Infantry Division

561st Volksgrenadier Division

Grossdeutchland Panzergrenadier Division

14th Infantry Division

Fortress Pillau LV Army Corps

50th Infantry Division

558th Volksgrenadier Division

286th Infantry Division

VI Army Corps

129th Infantry Division

170th Infantry Division

A Jagdpanzer IV which has been destroyed by Soviet artillery.

Fate of the German Forces in East Pomerania

IX Army Corps	This corps was commanded by General Rolf Wuthmann, who surrendered to the Soviets in the Samland April 20, 1945.
XVIII Mountain Corps	General Friedrich Hochbaum surrendered to the Soviets in the Weichselmünde in early May 1945.
XXIII Army Corps	General Walter Melzer surrendered to the Soviets May 8, 1945 in the Weichselmünde.
4th Panzer Division	General Clemens Betzel was killed in Danzig March 27, 1945. General Ernst-Wilhelm Hoffmann was commander of the division until April 1, 1945, and surrendered to the Red Army.
VII Panzer Corps	General Mortimer von Kessel surrendered to the Americans on May 2, 1945.
7th Panzer Division	General Karl Mauß was badly wounded on March 25, 1945, north of Danzig in the area of Oxhöft. He was then evacuated to Denmark. Also on March 25, General Hans Christern replaced Mauß. Remnants of the division were evacuated to Swinemünde in April 1945 and underwent a refit at Krampnitz. The division surrendered in May 1945.
73rd Infantry Division	Commanded by General Franz Schlieper. The divisional staff were evacuated from Hela on April 16, 1945, but most drowned with refugees onboard the freighter Goya. Remnants of the division were integrated in other units.
227th Infantry Division	General Ernst Ratz commanded the division until it was destroyed on the Tucheler Heide in West Prussia. Remnants of the division were transferred to Swinemünde in April 1945. The division and general surrendered in early May 1945.
542nd Volksgrenadier Division	General Karl Löwrick was killed in an accident in the Vistula bridgehead on April 8, 1945. Division disbanded during April 1945.
Division Hela East	General Eugen-Alexander Lobach was injured on April 9, 1945. Remnants of his division finally surrendered on May 9, 1945.
Fortress Division Danzig, January–March 1945	General Walter Freytag surrendered to the Soviets on May 8, 1945.
Gruppe Gümbel Fortress Gotenhafen	General Karl Gümbel surrendered to the Allies on May 10, 1945.
56th Infantry Division	Destroyed in the Heiligenbeil cauldron in March 1945. Remnants escaped to Pomerania.
102nd Infantry Division	Destroyed in the Heiligenbeil cauldron in March 1945. Remnants were absorbed by the 28th Jäger Division. Some units managed to retreat to Western Pomerania where they formed Division Gruppe 102.

131st Infantry Division	Destroyed in the Heiligenbeil cauldron in March 1945. Remnants escaped to Pomerania.
215th Infantry Division	Commanded by General Bruno Frankewitz, this division was destroyed in battles on the Tucheler Heide and Gotenhafen in March 1945. Remnants were absorbed into the 32nd Infantry Division in early April 1945, but Frankewitz was taken prisoner.
251st Infantry Division	The division was disbanded in March 1945. The staff were transferred to Swinemünde.
286th Infantry Division	Destroyed at Neukuhren in the Samland in April 1945. Remnants integrated to the 95th Infantry Division. Staff evacuated to Swinemünde in April 1945.
292nd Infantry-Division	Destroyed in the Heiligenbeil cauldron in March 1945. Remnants were integrated into the 170th Infantry Division in April 1945.
337th Volksgrenadier Division	Destroyed at Danzig. Remnants were integrated into 391st Defense Division. On April 11, 1945, the 319st was destroyed in the Halbe pocket.
349th Volksgrenadier Division	Destroyed in the Heiligenbeil cauldron in March 1945. Remnants were integrated into the 21st Infantry Division in April 1945.
389th Infantry Division	Defensive actions in Danzig and West Prussia. Division evacuated to Swinemünde in early April 1945.
541st Volksgrenadier Division	Division destroyed in Heiligenbeil cauldron in March 1945. Remnants evacuated to Swinemünde.
547th Volksgrenadier Division	Destroyed in East Prussia in late January 1945. Remnants were integrated into the 170th Infantry Division in February 1945.
549th Volksgrenadier Division	Destroyed in East Prussia in late January 1945. Remnants reformed at Pasewalk in Pomerania.
562nd Volksgrenadier Division	General Helmuth Hufenbach killed on March 27, 1945. The division was destroyed in the Heiligenbeil cauldron.
2nd Panzergrenadier Division Hermann Göring	Destroyed in Heiligenbeil cauldron in March 1945. Remnants evacuated in early April 1945.
18th Panzergrenadier Division	Destroyed in the Heiligenbeil cauldron. A new 18th Panzergrenadier Division was built from elements of the original in late March 1945.
24th Panzer Division	General Gustav-Adolf von Nostitz-Wallwitz was badly wounded on March 25, 1945, in the Heiligenbeil cauldron. The division was destroyed and saw Soviet forces clearing the remnants of German forces northeast of Berlin, allowing Zhukov's forces to finally launch the battle of Berlin from the Seelow Heights on the Oder on April 16, 1945.

Soviet soldiers inspecting a German Panther tank.

A T-34 bound for the Oder races past a column of trucks, April 1945.

Two photographs showing dejected and defeated German POWs being marched to the rear in late March/early April 1945. It is estimated that some three hundred and fifty thousand to four hundred thousand German troops were killed or captured in the East Pomerania operation. Some two hundred and thirty-four thousand were killed.

Further Reading

Batov, V. "Pokhadakh i Boyakh." *In Campaigns and Battles*. Moscow: Voenizdat, 1966.

Communist Party of the Soviet Union & Central Committee Institute of Marxism-Leninism. *Istoriya Velikoy Otechestvennoy Voyny Sovetskogo Soyuza, Vol. 3.* Moscow: Voennoe izdatelstvo Ministerstva Oborony Soyuza SSR, 1961.

Galitsan, A. S. *Chernigovsko-Pripyatskaya Operatsiya, Sovetskaya Voyennaya Entsiklopediya, Vol. 8.* Moscow: Voenizdat, 1980.

Garthoff, Raymond L. *How Russia Makes War: Soviet Military Doctrine* (Routledge Library Editions: Cold War Security Studies). Abingdon & New York: Routledge, 2001.

Glantz, David M. *Soviet Military Deception in the Second World War.* London: Frank Cass, 1989.

Glantz, David M. & House, Jonathan M. *When Titans Clashed: How the Red Army Stopped Hitler.* Lawrence: University of Kansas Press, 1995.

Glantz, David M. & Orenstein, Harold S. *Belorussia 1944: The Soviet General Staff Study.* London: Frank Cass Publishers, 2001.

Kieser, Egbert. *Prussian Apocalypse: The Fall of Danzig 1945.* Barnsley: Pen & Sword Books, 2011.

Le Tissier, Tony. *With Our Backs to Berlin: The Germany Army in Retreat 1945.* Brimscombe Port: The History Press, 2005.

Maclean, Fitzroy. *Eastern Approaches.* London: Penguin, 2009.

Soviet General Staff. *Prelude to Berlin: The Red Army's Offensive Operations in Poland and Eastern Germany, 1945.* Edited and translated by Richard W. Harrison. Solihull: Helion & Company in cooperation with the Association of the United States Army, 2016.

Timoshenko, S. K. "Closing Speech of the People's Commissar of Defense of the USSR." In David M. Glantz and Harold S. Orenstein, *The Evolution of Soviet Operational Art, 1927–1991: The Documentary Basis: Volume 1 (Operational Art 1927–1964) (Soviet Russian Study of War).* Abingdon & New York: Routledge, 1995.

Tucker-Jones, Anthony. *Slaughter on the Eastern Front: Hitler and Stalin's War 1941–1945.* Brimscombe Port: The History Press, 2017.

Hitlerjugend in 1945. Many of Hitler's fortresses were defended by Wehrmacht garrisons supported by a mixture of *Volkssturm* and Hitlerjugend conscripts, including local militia and volunteers.

Index